How to l
Christian

40 SIMPLE SPIRITUAL PRACTICES

Sally Welch

CANTERBURY
PRESS
Norwich

First published in 2016 by the Canterbury Press Norwich
Editorial office
3rd Floor, Invicta House
108–114 Golden Lane
London EC1Y 0TG, UK

Canterbury Press is an imprint of Hymns Ancient & Modern Ltd
(a registered charity)
13A Hellesdon Park Road, Norwich,
Norfolk NR6 5DR, UK

www.canterburypress.co.uk

Scripture quotations are from
The New International Version (NIV) copyright © 1973, 1978, 1984, 2011
by International Bible Society. Used by permission of Hodder & Stoughton
Ltd, a member of the Hodder Headline Ltd.
The New Revised Standard Version of the Bible, Anglicized Edition
(NRSV) copyright 1989, 1995, 2008 by the Division of Christian Education
of the National Council of the Churches of Christ in the USA.
Used by permission. All rights reserved.
The New King James Version. Copyright © 1982 by Thomas Nelson.
Used by permission. All rights reserved.

The publisher acknowledges with thanks permission to use copyright
owners' photographs. Wikimedia Commons images are used by a Creative
Commons Attribution-ShareAlike 3.0 licence.
p. 3: photo by www.commonswikimedia.org.
p. 93: photo by Michael O'Brian, Jesus Takes Up his Cross, www.studiobrien.com.
p. 121: photo by www.commons.wikimedia.org/wiki/File:Borce-2.jpg.

British Library Cataloguing in Publication data
A catalogue record for this book is available
from the British Library

978 1 84825 845 7

Typeset by Mary Matthews
Printed and bound in Great Britain by
CPI Group (UK) Ltd, Croydon, CR0 4YY

Contents

Introduction

Then little children were being brought to him in order that he might lay his hands on them and pray. The disciples spoke sternly to those who brought them; but Jesus said, 'Let the little children come to me, and do not stop them; for it is to such as these that the kingdom of heaven belongs.' And he laid his hands on them and went on his way.

Matthew 19.13–15

Jesus has been teaching in Galilee, telling huge crowds the good news of God's love for all people. He has just left the region and travelled to Judaea, but the crowds followed him there, eager to listen to his stories about the kingdom of heaven, to spend time with this man who knew so much about God and whose gifts for healing were becoming so well known. The disciples were trying to marshal the crowd, preventing Jesus from becoming swallowed up by the crush of people around him. They were probably trying to ensure that he met the right sort of people too: those with power and influence, those who could change the way things were run, the 'big hitters' in the area of religion. They were well meaning, this group of followers, but did not always understand – to them, the group of children and parents who clustered round Jesus were simply a nuisance. The little ones were getting in the way, perhaps their chatter and noise was preventing serious conversation and concentration on the important things. So, the disciples told them to go away. It would have been easy for Jesus not to have noticed these no doubt peremptory instructions to the supplicant parents; it would have been easy, if he had noticed them, for him to have ignored what was happening so that he might concentrate on the bigger picture. But for Jesus, these children were the bigger picture. He halted his discussion, his conversation, his interaction with the adults, the influencers, the decision makers, and he laid his hands upon the children; the young, the weak, the insignificant. '… it is to such as these that the kingdom of heaven belongs,' he proclaimed, and then he simply went on his way, leaving the crowd puzzling over his words and actions.

Something of the very essence of Christian mindfulness is evident in these few short verses, brief in words, but highly significant in content. A compassionate Christ notices those people who appear on the edge of life; the weak and vulnerable. His heart is filled with care for them and he shares with them the blessing of God, lifting them up as examples of those to whom the kingdom of heaven belongs, to the consternation and puzzlement of those who believe that the path to happiness lies in material goods, worldly success, power and status in society. None of these things matter to the child who lives each moment as it happens, rejoicing in the new discoveries made each moment; discoveries about their physical and mental abilities and about the world around them. The exterior world is perceived as an enchanting and fascinating place, full of opportunities to explore and learn to one who can bring their powers of concentration to focus on the smallest of objects – an insect or a flower. The interior world opens up new areas of possibility and interaction to the one who judges people on their attitude and nature, their approach to others and their care for themselves, rather than on the amount of wealth they possess or their position in society.

This book explores the nature of Christian mindfulness and offers an opportunity to reflect on various passages from the Bible that serve as springboards for prayer and contemplation. The reflections seek – through the medium of the five senses, and an examination of the Passion – to approach Christian living in a holistic and mindful way. Simple exercises are given at the end of each section to help open the door to a deeper understanding of God and a more mindful way of faith. Reflections are included for each day of Holy Week, so *How to be a Mindful Christian* can also be used as a Lent study companion if required.

The final chapter of the book – The Mindful Pilgrimage – offers thoughts and reflections on making a pilgrimage.

What is mindfulness?

Walking along any busy city street, it is difficult not to notice how many people look worried and anxious. So many of us live a frantic way of life that brings little satisfaction, perhaps driven by past memories or concerns about the future. The consumerist culture that promises fulfilment with the next purchase highlights the gap between the world that we strive towards and the world as we experience it. Driven by habit and automatic reactions practised for years, yet never held up to objective scrutiny, our default thought patterns are in danger of controlling our approach to the events of our lives, leaving us tense in mind and body, unable to focus clearly on the world as it is, seeing instead a vision of what we fear it may become.

The practice of mindfulness invites us to see the world just as it is, without judgement. It invites us to view our thoughts simply as events that occur in the mind, not as reality itself. We may notice our thoughts and their nature, observing whether they are negative or positive without becoming engaged with them or caught up in them. Mindfulness enables us to step off the treadmill of the past, and engage fully with the present. We learn not to anticipate events with anxiety or fear as we learn not to play out possible outcomes, but wait instead for the reality to unfold. We are encouraged to step outside the activity of our thoughts, to view them with compassion without engaging with them, noticing stress or unhappiness without feeling driven to act upon these emotions, but simply observing them. When we can accept reality as it is, just at this moment, we will be able to approach it in a more balanced way, without argument, confusion or impulsiveness but with awareness and clarity. This is wholly compatible with Christian faith, which encourages us to see ourselves as God sees us – with truthfulness, compassion and love.

We are all aware of the close relationship between the mind and the body. When the mind is stressed or unhappy, this is reflected in the level of tension in the body, which may develop into actual ill health. An awareness of this link opens the way to an engagement with it; conscious relaxation of the muscles and sinews of the body can ease physical pain and mental pressure. This interested, detached approach, which is at the same time compassionate and yet freed from emotional associations, can be directed outwards, towards the physical world that surrounds us. Mindfulness invites us to encounter the physical world apprehended by our senses with curiosity and excitement, noticing the environment that we inhabit, approaching it with interest, directing our focus towards the everyday activities of our lives in a way that enhances our awareness of our surroundings and provides a sense of perspective which gives proportion and balance to our experiences. With renewed confidence in our judgements of the world around us, we are able to remember the past and plan for the future without being trapped by either. Our experiences are precious and provide a resource of wisdom and expertise; our imaginations enable us to dream and be creative, but these are merely tools for engaging with reality rather than reality itself.

A mindful approach to life enables us to pause, to step outside our own heads and engage with the real outside world with all its fascinating charm. We are invited to become more aware of ourselves and of others, to cherish our whole selves, and appreciate the rich variety of our inner life, our sadnesses as well as our joys, appreciating and accepting our emotions with compassion and acknowledging them without becoming defined by them.

The practitioner of mindfulness adopts a holistic approach to life, which enables them to receive with gratitude the kaleidoscope of experience which is available to those who are open to the present moment. Mindful meditation opens up spaces in our lives and heads which offer the opportunity to think and feel differently, which give the freedom to choose the best way to solve problems. Pauses, breaths and moments of stillness prevent us from becoming inseparable from our emotions, clearing our minds and enabling us to see reality. In this way we will in turn be able to offer compassion to others, patient with their faults just as we have learnt to be patient with our own, accepting our flaws while refusing to be defined by them, and sharing this empathy with others.

Christian mindfulness

It is a warm afternoon in July. A group of people has gathered on a terrace outside a cathedral on a hill overlooking a large city. Below them the city is set out like a child's drawing, the straight streets filled with houses, tiny trees and traffic moving in fits and starts as it pauses briefly at crossroads before joining the flow again. The noise of the city is faint from the viewpoint of the onlookers – among them is a silence that is full of expectation. On the terrace a complicated pattern is laid out in beautiful stone slabs; it twists and turns around a central rose, and if the eye follows closely the curves and bends of the pattern, it will be seen to consist of just one path, beginning at the outer edge of the pattern and opening out into the central petals.

One by one the people approach the entry of the path, pause, then begin slowly to walk, following the line of coloured stones as they weave among each other. It is almost as if these people were dancing – a slow, graceful dance, full of thought and feeling. Some of the walkers pause when they arrive at the centre, standing still or sitting or kneeling, facing towards the cathedral or looking out over the city. Others simply turn immediately and retrace their steps towards the outer edge of the pattern. As they walk, the people appear to become calmer; their steps slow, their breathing deepens. Eyes carefully focused on the pathway ahead of them, some will pause to look up, others stop in their tracks, eyes fixed on the ground. Finally, each member of the group has walked the entire path from the outside to the central rose then back out again, and has taken up a position around the outside of the pattern. When all are still once more, a prayer is said, and the group disperses.

They have just walked the labyrinth, and, in the midst of a busy city, have encountered the stillness and calm that comes from focusing simply on the moment. Letting go of memories of the past and anticipation of the future, they have concentrated simply on the physical and mental experiences of the moment itself, content to allow it to be what it is, without judging or criticizing. For a brief time, the walkers have ceased their mental commentary on the events that surround them and allowed themselves purely to exist, noticing internal and external feelings and sensations without giving them energy, being aware of their bodies as they move through the labyrinth, noticing how this movement feels and its effect on their emotions. Freed from the baggage of the past and a preoccupation with the future, the walkers have found the space they need for creativity and imagination, for interaction with the moment itself as it happens, in all its preciousness. In the moment of the now, God is to be found. God, who exists outside time, who is eternity itself, allows us to encounter eternity in the immediate.

Throughout the Bible, we are reminded of the fact that we will never encounter God if we are so preoccupied with ourselves that there is no room for anything else. We are taught to set aside our thoughts and feelings to make space for God, to allow the love of God for us to fill our hearts and minds so that we are no longer preoccupied with the past or afraid for the future, but simply content to dwell with God in his love through his grace. Jesus, in his struggle in the desert, does not argue with Satan, simply sets what he says aside. He does not allow his thoughts and feelings to be kidnapped by a preoccupation with his reaction to the temptations of wealth and power; he acknowledges them, but treats them merely as the passing of an inconvenient weather system over the mountain of God's eternal and unmoving love. In Martha's resentful busyness, her need to be needed and appreciated, we see the perils of not being present to the moment, of allowing expectation and past experience to cloud the appreciation of the moments of companionship and the presence of Christ. In Mary's calm enjoyment we observe the joy of the 'now', the relishing of precious moments, freed from clouds of obligation and past patterns into the open space of the new. When our attention is removed from the necessity of anticipating every event, of plundering the past to provide new sources of anxiety for the future, we will be able to see things for what they are, in the intensity of their beauty, in the perfection of their creation. Emotions will no longer enslave us, and in the freedom into which we have been released, we will encounter God. Once we have ceased to allow our thoughts to be shaped by patterns from the past, they can be transformed (Romans 12.2). Christian mindfulness enables us to move away from negative ways of thinking and adopt new habits of thought, ones that enable us to focus on the moment, to derive strength from the knowledge that good or bad, the experiences of the now are the ones that shape us and reshape us, enabling us to see and hear again. The sacrament of the present moment is the doorway to the eternal and universal; an acknowledgement of our physicality leads to an appreciation of ourselves as embodied people, whose lives have been transformed by the Word made flesh. When our minds connect with our environment, we can make the whole of creation part of our prayer, recognizing that God can be found in every detail of the landscape, his unique loving signature within every living creature.

Once we can appreciate each moment, each object for what it is, we will cease to become burdened by our judgements upon these things. Pure enjoyment in all things, in all moments, will liberate us from a preoccupation with having, gaining, achieving, possessing. Mindful prayer releases us simply to reflect upon the moment, not relying on our possession of it to validate it or ourselves but simply to experience it, free from the chains of thoughts that habit drapes around the most commonplace actions. 'We are God's children now' (1 John 3.2), and it is in the now, and only in the now, that we can truly serve God because it is in this moment that we are met by him. Freed from the past and the preoccupations of the past we can forgive the past and allow ourselves to be forgiven. Open to future events we can cease our hopeless attempts to protect ourselves from it in the shape of possessions, status or power. We will not be able to avoid the storm, perhaps, but we will no longer be threatened by it, because we face reality in the strength we are given by God. The 'sign of Jonah' found in Luke 11.29 is perhaps the knowledge that is the fruit of the acceptance of suffering with a calm mind, unafraid and clear of purpose. Willingly giving up our defended state, we join Christ at the foot of the cross, prepared to face suffering but not to be overwhelmed by it, observing it detachedly within the love of God.

Mindful prayer enables us to be receptive to the whole world because we refuse to be captured by it. No longer fearful for our own safety, we are secure in our knowledge that Jesus took our place on the cross so that we could take his place in the kingdom. From this security we can reach out to others, no longer labelling them but loving them, free to serve because we no longer need to be served or to be defined by the judgement of others. Honouring ourselves, with our flaws and faults, will free us to honour others, seeing them objectively but with compassion, our clear-sightedness not masked by our own insecurity. Honouring God within us will enable us to honour God beyond us.

The space that mindful meditation releases within us reveals that this space is shot through with Christ. We are the deep that we call to (Psalm 42.7), as Christ dwells within us. Once we are aware of the infinite outside ourselves, we will be aware of it within:

To see a World in a Grain of Sand
And a Heaven in a Wild Flower
Hold Infinity in the palm of your hand
And Eternity in an hour.
      William Blake, 'Auguries of Innocence'

Soul you must seek yourself in Me
and in yourself seek Me.
　　Teresa of Avila, 'Seeking God'

So I tell you, whatever you ask for in prayer, believe that
you have received it, and it will be yours.
　　　　　　　　　　　　　　　　　　　Mark 11.24

Through mindful prayer, we start from where we are and with what we have, and we discover that we have already reached our destination for we journey with Christ, our companion and our goal. If we release ourselves from the internal running commentary that is the backdrop to our lives, we will discover stillness. Within that stillness, we will find an attention to the moment, to the now, in its purest form. Within that 'now' we will find God.

Let this presence settle into your bones, and allow your soul
the freedom to sing, dance, praise and love.
　　　　　　　　　　　　　　　　　　Teresa of Avila

40 Days of Mindfulness

THE SENSES

This first section of reflections is offered as a way of experiencing and practising mindful prayer. They are set out in a way that honours our senses, those five ways in which we experience the external world. Through the medium of sight, taste, smell, sound and touch you are invited to engage with different aspects of mindful prayer, noticing also the way that the various aspects of mindfulness run like threads throughout the Bible. A selection of Old and New Testament readings are offered, as well as prayers from the Psalms.

The reflections begin with an introduction to mindful meditation, explored through the theme of silence.

SILENCE

'I Am'
EXODUS 3.14, 15

> *God said to Moses, 'I Am who I Am.' He said further, 'Thus you shall say to the Israelites, 'I Am has sent me to you.'*

Moses has had a life full of incident. Saved from slaughter as an infant by the ingenuity of his mother, he is adopted by the Pharaoh's daughter and spent his childhood and youth enjoying the consequent privileges. But he remains a Hebrew at heart, and in an overflow of righteous anger kills one of those who sought to harm his people. When news of this action reaches Pharaoh, Moses flees for his life. His time of wealth and ease is over and in his new life as a shepherd Moses settles down into obscurity. But God's people groan under the power of the Egyptians and God 'took notice of them' (Exodus 2.25). Moses is chosen by God to bring his people out of Egypt but he hesitates, seeking further instructions – why should the Hebrew people follow him, a mere shepherd, a murderer, an outlaw? So God tells Moses under whose authority he will act – that of God himself. 'I Am has sent me to you'. The Hebrew word is YHWH. It has no vowels; it is but a breath, the merest expiration, no more than a sigh. But it is the breath that gives us life that sustains us, without which we would perish. From that first breath of God over the chaos of the universe, when the spirit of God 'swept over the face of the waters' (Genesis 1.2), we have been sustained and supported by the breath of creation, of love, the sighing of YHWH who murmurs 'I Am' into our troubled turbulent lives, breathing peace and calm, reminding us of his presence, his love.

Just as God takes 'notice' of the groaning of his people under the weight of their slavery in Egypt, so too does his eye fall upon us, and he takes notice. No care or difficulty is too small for him, no injury or anxiety escapes his mindful eye, for God notices and into them he breathes his spirit, healing and redeeming. But the relationship is not one-sided, for although God takes notice and acts, he chooses to do so through the agency of one of his people, who must join with him in the act of noticing. The work of rescue is a partnership, a covenant between God and Moses. The burning bush is placed as a sign for Moses, but he must turn aside from the daily tasks and investigate this phenomenon. He must not allow himself to be so caught up in the necessary busyness of physical survival that he fails to notice the task of his soul. Once he has his attention, God speaks to Moses and invites him into partnership with him for the freedom of his people, but Moses feels unworthy, afraid 'who am I that I should go?' God must remind him that he is not alone, that the task is not solely his but the work of God himself. Further reassurance is given in the authority of God's name – the creative, redemptive breath that gives life to a suffocating world.

EXERCISE

You will probably at some time today discover that you are feeling busy, anxious, or even stressed. It would be wonderful if you didn't and, if this is the case, give thanks that you don't need to do this exercise! However, the majority of us will feel under pressure at some time or another and, like the people of Israel, will 'groan' under our burden of care and worry. When this happens, take a short breathing space; it need be no more than three minutes.

Find a comfortable place to sit or lie – if this is not possible, find somewhere you can stand undisturbed for a short time. Make sure you feel supported and balanced in your body, relaxed but alert. Close your eyes if this helps. Take some time to take 'notice' of what is happening in your mind right now. You don't need to comment on it or judge or decide on any action, simply be aware of the thoughts and worries that are churning about. Do not allow yourself to become engaged with them; just observe them.

Now move your attention to your breath, feeling it enter and leave your body, filling your body with life. Focus on the breath as it moves in and out. If your mind wanders, do not become anxious or concerned, simply take notice and return to the breath, in and out.

On your out breath you might like to breathe the word YHWH, allowing it to become part of your exhalation. Let the breath become your prayer, your answering call to the reassurance and love of the breath of God as it fills your whole body; 'This is my name for ever, and this my title for all generations' (Exodus 3.15).

Restoring the soul
PSALM 23

> The Lord is my shepherd, I shall not want.
> He makes me lie down in green pastures;
> he leads me beside still waters;
>   he restores my soul.
> He leads me in right paths
>   for his name's sake.
>
> Even though I walk through the darkest valley,
>   I fear no evil;
> for you are with me;
>   your rod and your staff –
>   they comfort me.

You prepare a table before me
   in the presence of my enemies;
you anoint my head with oil;
   my cup overflows.
Surely goodness and mercy shall follow me
   all the days of my life,
and I shall dwell in the house of the Lord
   my whole life long.

This psalm is probably the best known and most loved part of the Bible, second only to the Lord's Prayer for its familiarity even for those who know no other portions. It is a triumph of peace and certainty amid disturbing and uncertain times. It contains a calmness and confidence in the love of the good shepherd, who leads his sheep to the places where they can best find shelter and rest. He encourages his flock to 'lie down' – not to spend too much time rushing around aimlessly in a panic, but instead to put down the burdens and anxieties of life and take proper rest. The sheep are led beside 'still waters' so that they can be completely nourished in both body and soul, refreshed with cool water and encouraged by the beauty of the landscape that surrounds them.

The pace of the psalm is slow and measured; enjoyment and ease in the whole body – as well as the soul – flows throughout the first few verses. But then a change occurs, because although we, the flock of the good shepherd, are led in the 'right paths', these paths seem to take us through the 'darkest valley[s]'. Surely this was not what we signed up for when we became Christians? We looked for peace, for love, for forgiveness, for hope, for light – certainly not for dark valleys. And yet there are occasions in our lives when we seem to be surrounded by darkness, and then we are confused and frightened. Too often the temptation is to act just like sheep in a panic, skittering here and there aimlessly, achieving nothing but becoming dangerously upset, to the detriment of the entire community

7

in which we live. But sometimes, in order to reach new, safer places, where there is more nourishment, where perhaps the lush grass of the meadows has not all been eaten but new, fresh grazing places are to be found to sustain us, we must be led through dark valleys. Just as in the landscape, fertile valleys are separated from one another by narrow passes that are difficult to navigate, so to move from one stage of life to another, one level of understanding to a deeper one, may bring about difficulties and disturbance.

There may be times when it seems as if God is far away, as if we have been led into dark places and there abandoned, but this psalm echoes the loving reassurance with which the whole of the Bible is filled – God will never leave us, he always has a purpose for us, and that purpose is always good, although we may not always understand it. We need not be afraid, for the good shepherd is always with us, protecting us and caring for us and, because of that, we may be sure that we will be surrounded by goodness and mercy all the days of our lives.

EXERCISE

The body scan can be used to focus our minds away from the relentless activity that they produce, endlessly constructing possible scenarios or trying out different strategies, playing out future events in numerous different ways, often based on past experiences that colour present emotions and prevent us from seeing our situation clearly, compassionately but objectively. By focusing on our bodies, we can anchor ourselves in the present moment, giving us a breathing space in which to take stock of our thoughts and feelings and see them for what they are, rather than becoming overwhelmed by them and accepting them as a reality that is often far different. We can connect once more with our physical selves, becoming aware of the ways in which our bodies react to emotional disturbance.

We can put a stop to a spiral of negative thoughts and detach ourselves from them, separating them from reality in a loving way that allows us to see them for what they are. We can give ourselves time to remember the loving kindness of the good shepherd, and restore our faith in his leadership and confidence in his care for us, restoring our own faith in our ability to deal with our situation realistically and calmly.

Find a quiet space where you can be still and comfortable. This can be sitting or lying, but it should be somewhere you can be still for a sustained period of time. Settle yourself so that you will remain alert and aware, and slow your breathing, gradually becoming aware of your physical surroundings – where your body touches your chair, or the surface on which you are lying, how you feel within your clothes.

Beginning with your toes, try to discern any sensation or feeling in them. Don't worry if you feel nothing, sometimes this comes with continued practice of the body scan. If you feel discomfort in your toes, notice this. Try not to become involved in analysing the sensation or worrying about it, simply notice it without judging, allowing it to be what it is. Deepen your breathing, becoming aware of your breath flowing throughout your entire body, filling every blood cell with oxygen, sustaining life.

Gradually move your attention from your toes to your feet, then to the lower and upper parts of your legs. Steadily and slowly, focus on each part of your body in turn, resting your attention on it for ten or twenty seconds, without deliberately counting the time, simply pausing long enough to register the sensations that you feel. If you experience tension or pain, breathe into them, exploring the feeling, allowing your mind to register the feeling without judging it, simply noticing it, before moving on.

Don't worry if your mind wanders – it probably will. When it does, simply bring it back to the task in hand, the task of the present, and continue your journey round your body.

After you have scanned your whole body, continue breathing in silence, aware of your body as a whole, loved by God, part of the unique individual that he formed for his loving purpose. You may want to pray Psalm 23, breathing the first half of each verse on the in breath and the second part on the out.

Abide in me
JOHN 15.1–11

'I am the true vine, and my Father is the vinegrower. He removes every branch in me that bears no fruit. Every branch that bears fruit he prunes to make it bear more fruit. You have already been cleansed by the word that I have spoken to you. Abide in me as I abide in you. Just as the branch cannot bear fruit by itself unless it abides in the vine, neither can you unless you abide in me. I am the vine, you are the branches. Those who abide in me and I in them bear much fruit, because apart from me you can do nothing. Whoever does not abide in me is thrown away like a branch and withers; such branches are gathered, thrown into the fire, and burned. If you abide in me, and my words abide in you, ask for whatever you wish, and it will be done for you. My Father is glorified by this, that you bear much fruit and become my disciples. As the Father has loved me, so I have loved you; abide in my love. If you keep my commandments, you will abide in my love, just as I have kept my Father's commandments and abide in his love. I have said these things to you so that my joy may be in you, and that your joy may be complete.'

This passage contains one of the great 'I Am' sayings of Jesus, using the rich language of metaphor to help his listeners understand not only who he is, but how our relationship with him should be seen. We are encouraged to see ourselves as sheep, cared for by a loving shepherd and, even more deeply, as the branches of the vine who gain support and sustenance from the strong central trunk. And we need this reassurance, we need this strength to hold on to in our daily lives, as we struggle to retain awareness of the peace of Christ that lies in the depths of our souls. For there is peace, and great love, at the heart of our relationship with God in Christ, if we allow ourselves to be transformed by him, if we let him enter our lives and show us new ways to live, new ways to think and speak and act. This is not easy work, as our former way of life can seem entrancingly simple and engagingly easy, with the necessity only to conform to the ways of the world, rather than the more demanding way of love which is Christ's message to us. We must learn to be still, to seek to abide in Christ, rather than to seek continually for the next new thrill, the next challenge, the next possession dangled in front of us by the shrill materialism of the secular world. We must look to root ourselves securely into the heart of the vine, taking nourishment from a love so deep that it can never be plumbed, so all-encompassing that it can never be extinguished, so forgiving that the ends of its mercy will never be reached. Henry Francis Lyte's famous hymn 'Abide with me', based on Jesus' encounter with the disciples on the road to Emmaus (Luke 24.13–35), contains the line 'come not to sojourn but abide with me'. Christ's invitation to us is simply to allow ourselves to experience his love, and to find within it all that we need, abiding in him as he abides in us.

EXERCISE

Find a place to be still and quiet. Make yourself comfortable, either sitting or lying, with your eyes open or closed, as you prefer. Still your mind and body, using the three-minute breathing exercise. Then simply picture yourself resting in God's arms. You can imagine yourself as a small child or as the fully grown person you are now. Imagine the sensations of being held by God; the warmth and comfort of his arms, the security of his grasp. Imagine his great love for you surrounding and enveloping you in its forgiving warmth and understanding. Pray for yourself, that you may remain aware of God's great love for you, and his peace that is always available to you. Try to set aside your concerns about yourself and what you do, who you are, and instead simply enjoy being in God's presence. You could pray on an in breath: 'May I find peace', or 'May I be happy' or simply 'God is with me'. Try not to let your mind dwell on your actions or words, simply on the fact of being a child of God, God's creation. When you are ready, focus again on the sensation of the breath entering and leaving your body.

God's children now
1 JOHN 3.1–3

> *See what love the Father has given us, that we should be called children of God; and that is what we are. The reason the world does not know us is that it did not know him. Beloved, we are God's children now; what we will be has not yet been revealed. What we do know is this: when he is revealed, we will be like him, for we will see him as he is. And all who have this hope in him purify themselves, just as he is pure.*

'We are God's children now', writes John. We do not have to wait for God's love, or earn the right to be called his children; all this is ours already. Our task is simply to rejoice in that love and share it so that our full potential as children of God can be realized. Ours is not to fret about the future, but instead to celebrate the miracle of the incarnate God, the miracle of God's compassionate awareness and loving acceptance poured into each moment, enfolding us in a love that will hold us securely – as it always has done and as it will continue to do, into eternity.

In the focused discipline of bringing God's presence to mind continually throughout the day there will be found the joyful rewards of taking whatever opportunity we can to dedicate our actions to God. We will experience a changed attitude to the world and to ourselves as we appreciate the gift of love that is in God, in the immediate moment.

One of the most significant changes that will occur will be that of our relationship with other people. The first letter of John is full of admonitions and exhortations to love one another. John knows that the task of loving an invisible God, whose actions can sometimes only be intuited and whose behaviour is often misunderstood and directions unclear, is a challenging one. But he knows that even more demanding is the obligation made upon each one of us not just to love God, but to love those who share our daily lives – people whose presence is sometimes only too obvious, whose behaviour is often deeply unhelpful and whose company can be challenging and uncomfortable. None the less, these are the people whom we have been given to love, whom it is a duty and a joy to care for, who will grow in Christ with us. Always, together with the injunction to love God, is coupled the command to love one another, as we love ourselves, thus giving us a twofold duty towards our own selves and the members of our family and wider community.

EXERCISE

Find a place to be still and quiet. Make yourself comfortable, either sitting or lying, with your eyes open or closed, as you prefer. Still your mind and body, using the three-minute breathing exercise. Then bring to mind a person with whom you share your life, and whom you love or care for. They do not have to be the person you are most fond of, or the person you find most difficult to live alongside. Imagine this person in the shelter of God's loving arms, encircled by his love. Imagine the warmth and comfort of his arms, the security of his grasp. Imagine his great love for the person surrounding them and enveloping them in its forgiving warmth and understanding. Pray for them, that they may remain aware of God's great love for them, and his peace that is always available to them. Try to set aside what you know or think you know about the person, and allow them simply to rest in God's arms. Try not to focus on their characteristics or to bring to mind their words or actions, but simply hold them before God in your heart. If your mind becomes distracted, or wanders off, remembering incidents or conversations, do not worry about this. Simply acknowledge that your mind has wandered and become too focused on small details, and bring it back to the present moment, enjoying the company of God in the person you are focusing on. Do not worry if you do not feel particularly aware of God's presence or if your feelings about the person are ambivalent or unchanged; simply notice this and continue to focus, remembering that they, with you, are one of God's children now. You could pray on an in breath: 'May you find peace', or 'May you be happy' or simply 'God is with you'. When you are ready, focus again on the sensation of the breath entering and leaving your body.

Cherishing challenging people
REVELATION 8.1–4

When the Lamb opened the seventh seal, there was silence in heaven for about half an hour. And I saw the seven angels who stand before God, and seven trumpets were given to them.

Another angel with a golden censer came and stood at

the altar; he was given a great quantity of incense to offer with the prayers of all the saints on the golden altar that is before the throne. And the smoke of the incense, with the prayers of the saints, rose before God from the hand of the angel.

The readers of John's book of Revelation have been amazed and disturbed by its contents for thousands of years. The colourful symbolism, the light touch the writer has concerning the matter of chronology, the disconcertingly rapid alterations of viewpoint, the highly dramatic events that unfold from between the pages of the book, all add to a sense of colourful turbulence that none the less contains enormous assurance as to the outcome of the challenges and battles that are being described. And the original readers of the book must have longed for that reassurance. Written, as we know, to the seven churches of Asia, the book was both a means of instruction in the ways of being a Christian community, and a source of comfort in the face of the incredible persecution the early Christians were experiencing at that time. Struggling to live in a new and profoundly challenging way, one that turned on its head all previous notions of the appropriate way to live and upset many of society's accepted norms and values, these fledgling communities were not even left in peace to wrestle with the issues of living together in Christ. Instead they faced determined and bitter opposition and persecution from religious and state authorities alike. How tiring it must have been to live in constant fear for one's life, not knowing whether the day will bring news of the imprisonment and torture of a friend or family member, or one's own capture. How they must have suffered times of doubt and unbelief, as their desperate prayers went unanswered and yet another Christian family was either slaughtered or forced to recant. Into the darkness of these days, the colourful imagery and action of Revelation shines out like a torch, with its message of hope illuminating the bleak landscape of despair. 'Do not give up' – the book positively sings its message. Undoubtedly the world is full of evil at the moment, and much adversity is being suffered by the followers of Christ. This is because Satan's attempt to overthrow God and take over the kingdom of heaven has already failed. Satan has already been defeated, but he is still trying to attack God, this time through the medium of God's people. But evil still stalks the earth, and the skirmishes that this provokes are real and bitter, the war itself is over, and God has triumphed. So Christians must face persecution and difficulty, but can do so in the knowledge that the kingdom of heaven is already present and that death has already been defeated. In the meantime, they must continue to work at the very real task of becoming truly Christian communities, keeping to the right path, continuing to share the gospel in love and peace, striving to live together in harmony. None of these are easy tasks, even for Christians living without threat of persecution, and there must have been times when they wondered whether their prayers were being heard at all, never mind actually answered. But Revelation provides reassurance for this as well – the vision of heaven in worship provides an idea of the place of the prayers of the people in the glory of God. All prayers are offered up before the throne with incense in silence. Dignity and weight are given to them, and we are left in no doubt that they will be heard.

EXERCISE

Most of us are fortunate enough not to experience undue suffering for the fact of being Christian. However, that does not liberate us from the many challenges of Christian living, particularly that of living in community with or alongside fellow human beings, many of whom we may find challenging or even unpleasant, their actions causing us unhappiness or harm. This exercise provides a way of holding people that we find difficult to be with, wishing them well without giving in to their demands, trying to love them without allowing them to hurt us, pausing for a moment to step aside from our own relationship with them, and simply pray for their wellbeing.

Find a place to be still and quiet. Make yourself comfortable, either sitting or lying, with your eyes open or closed, as you prefer. Still your mind and body, using the three-minute breathing exercise. Then bring to your attention a person whom you find difficult or challenging. They do not have to be the most unpleasant person you deal with or anyone whom you find too upsetting to contemplate, simply a person who causes you mild annoyance. Imagine them cradled in the hand of God, being held and supported by him, cared for by him out of his great love. Try to set aside your feelings about them and simply pray for them, that they may be happy and at peace. You could pray on an in breath, addressing them directly: 'May you find peace' or 'May you be happy' or simply 'God is with you'. Try not to let your mind dwell on the actions or words of the person, or your relationship with them – simply on the fact of their being a child of God, God's creation. When you are ready, leave them with God and focus again on the sensation of the breath entering and leaving your body.

A mindful walk
MARK 1.35–38

In the morning, while it was still very dark, he got up and went out to a deserted place, and there he prayed. And Simon and his companions hunted for him. When they found him, they said to him, 'Everyone is searching for you.' He answered, 'Let us go on to the neighbouring towns, so that I may proclaim the message there also; for that is what I came out to do.'

If you were to look at a map of Galilee, with the journeyings of Jesus traced out upon it, you would find it criss-crossed with trail lines. If those that had been travelled more than once were coloured in a more vivid hue, some of those trail lines would be very bright indeed, for the ministry of Jesus – although it took place in one small area of the world – was full of movement. From the beginning, Jesus freed himself from the ties of property and place, enabling himself to move from town to village, healing and teaching where there was a need, rather than where he had been put under obligation by domestic necessity. He proclaims this lack of attachment to place eloquently: 'Foxes have dens and birds have nests, but the Son of Man has no place to lay his head' (Luke 9.58). Even the wildest of creatures, the desert fox, shelters in a den, and the bird soaring into the skies returns to a nest each night, but this is not a possibility for the one whose purpose on earth is to free those who are held captive, and release those who are bound. Christ was driven by two things – the imperative to 'proclaim the message' to all who needed to hear it meant that he journeyed through settlements, villages and towns, visiting synagogues, sharing meals, holding open air meetings for anyone who would listen. However, in order to find the energy and discern the purpose behind his mission, he had also to journey away from the presence of people, into the wild and deserted places, to meet God and to listen to him. It was in the wilderness that Christ encountered God and found the strength to fulfil his purpose. For him this was a primary duty, more than a duty, a nourishing, sustaining activity without which no secondary activity would be effective. Again and again in the Gospels, we find references to Jesus going away to pray, finding a quiet place to be with God, stepping aside from the pressures of teaching and healing to find strength in prayer and a renewal of relationship with his Father. He climbed hills, walked along shorelines, took boats across lakes, seeking silent places where he could find the space to remember and reinforce his purpose, reclaiming it for himself, and ensuring that he was not distracted by the agendas and aims of others but remained true to himself and to God.

So too we can find in purposeful, mindful movement a reassurance and reaffirmation of ourselves and our place in this world, a reminder of our place within the order of created things and a celebration of our earthly existence.

EXERCISE

If at all possible, take a mindful journey somewhere today to a quiet place. Ideally this would be a walk in silence to an isolated and peaceful spot where you can be alone, but if this is not possible, you could travel on your own to an unfamiliar place where you will not be recognized and distracted by the necessity of conversation or social interaction with others. Take a bus or train journey, travelling courteously but with a distance between you and your fellow travellers, wrapping yourself in silence. Find a quiet spot – churches and chapels are the ideal places, as every effort is made in even the most popular of cathedrals to set aside a place for private prayer. Walk slowly and purposefully to your chosen place, aware of every movement that your body makes, celebrating in its ability to make such actions. Try and focus your attention on different parts of your body as you walk, concentrating first on your feet and the sensation of walking on the ground, the type of surface, and the feeling of this underfoot. Move your attention slowly upwards, feeling your calf and thigh muscles stretch and contract as you take each step, the action of your chest as it draws breath, your arms by your side or gently swinging in time with each pace. If any part of your body registers discomfort or pain, notice this, and stay with it briefly, inhabiting that part of the body without concerning yourself overmuch; simply registering the feeling. On your arrival at your destination, spend some time in silence, in a posture that is comfortable and relaxed, feeling the sensation of fabric, wood, stone, against parts of your body, allowing your mind the space simply to be a child of God, loved by God, in all your bodily form, with all its personal characteristics and idiosyncrasies. You might want to use your breathing prayer (see page 6), or even a whole body scan (page 8), during your time in silence.

When you have spent as long as you need or are able, return home slowly and mindfully once more, focusing on the feelings of movement and acknowledging your place in the environment you travel through.

SOUND

Objective listening
1 SAMUEL 3.1–18

Now the boy Samuel was ministering to the Lord under Eli. The word of the Lord was rare in those days; visions were not widespread.

At that time Eli, whose eyesight had begun to grow dim so that he could not see, was lying down in his room; the lamp of God had not yet gone out, and Samuel was lying down in the temple of the Lord, where the ark of God was. Then the Lord called, 'Samuel! Samuel!' and he said, 'Here I am!' and ran to Eli, and said, 'Here I am, for you called me.' But he said, 'I did not call; lie down again.' So he went and lay down. The Lord called again, 'Samuel!' Samuel got up and went to Eli, and said, 'Here I am, for you called me.' But he said, 'I did not call, my son; lie down again.' Now Samuel did not yet know the Lord, and the word of the Lord had not yet been revealed to him. The Lord called Samuel again, a third time. And he got up and went to Eli, and said, 'Here I am, for you called me.' Then Eli perceived that the Lord was calling the boy. Therefore Eli said to Samuel, 'Go, lie down; and if he calls you, you shall say, "Speak, Lord, for your servant is listening."' So Samuel went and lay down in his place.

Now the Lord came and stood there, calling as before, 'Samuel! Samuel!' And Samuel said, 'Speak, for your servant is listening.' Then the Lord said to Samuel, 'See, I am about to do something in Israel that will make both ears of anyone who hears of it tingle. On that day I will fulfil against Eli all that I have spoken concerning his house, from beginning to end. For I have told him that I am about to punish his house for ever, for the iniquity that he knew, because his sons were blaspheming God, and he did not restrain them. Therefore I swear to the house of Eli that the iniquity of Eli's house shall not be expiated by sacrifice or offering for ever.'

Samuel lay there until morning; then he opened the doors of the house of the Lord. Samuel was afraid to tell the vision to Eli. But Eli called Samuel and said, 'Samuel, my son.' He said, 'Here I am.' Eli said, 'What was it that he told you? Do not hide it from me. May God do so to you and more also, if you hide anything from me of all that he told you.' So Samuel told him everything and hid nothing from him. Then he said, 'It is the Lord; let him do what seems good to him.'

This story hinges on the most incredible obedience, not only of Samuel but also of Eli. It shows a complete readiness to follow the commands of God, whatever they may be, and as such is a demonstration of such faith in God's loving purposes for his people that we can only marvel at it. But prior to this, the story examines what it is actually to listen to God, to hear his call, however unusual this may be, to pay close attention to what God is saying, and then to act on it.

It is interesting that we learn that 'visions were not widespread' in those days. This gives the impression that worship, although it was being performed, was perhaps not the prime focus of the children of Israel. A lack of visions indicates that the Israelites were following the path of God as closely as they could have been, as we have already learnt earlier. Because they have strayed far from God, they cannot hear his voice, and they do not have visions. Samuel himself, we are told, does not yet 'know the Lord'; we must presume he was acting merely as Eli's servant, rather than as his assistant in the temple. Samuel it is who hears God's voice, but does not know that is what he is hearing; it is Eli who understands and gives Samuel the appropriate instructions. It is Eli who is brave enough to listen to the message that God has for him, delivered through Samuel, and it is Eli who accepts that message, doom-laden though it is. Eli knows he has done wrong, and is prepared to accept the consequences – it is only by doing so that he put himself right by God. His words in the face of his punishment are among the most courageous in the Bible, although they are rarely acclaimed as such: 'It is the Lord; let him do what seems good to him.'

There are times in our lives when disaster strikes, for whatever reason and in whatever way, whether it is deserved or not, expected or totally out of the blue. The mindful Christian trusts in God's loving purposes for their life and, in doing so, gains the courage to gaze directly on the problem, seeing it as it is, without trying to escape or evade it, but equally without investing it with emotion or energy which is unnecessary. In this way, we can save our resources for tackling the issue directly, rather than the emotions and memories that the issue might have stirred up.

EXERCISE

When you have a difficult conversation with a person, try to detach yourself from your feelings about what they are saying and actually pay close attention to their words. Try not to invest their speech with your own interpretations, coloured by your moods and memories of previous encounters with the person, but to listen as if for the first time to what they are saying. If you find it hostile or upsetting, register that this is what you are feeling without becoming involved; simply notice the feeling and allow it to pass by. Try to feel loving kindness for the person you are talking to, and for yourself.

The awakened ear
ISAIAH 50.4–6

> *The Lord God has given me*
> *The tongue of the learned,*
> *That I should know how to speak*
> *A word in season to him who is weary.*
> *He awakens me morning by morning,*
> *He awakens my ear*
> *To hear as the learned.*
> *The Lord God has opened my ear;*
> *And I was not rebellious,*
> *Nor did I turn away.*
> *I gave my back to those who struck me,*
> *And my cheeks to those who plucked out the beard;*
> *I did not hide my face from shame and spitting.*

The children of Israel are complaining bitterly against what they perceive as their abandonment by God. It was the people who turned away from God, and now find themselves in the wilderness. But God has had pity on them, and sends his prophet to comfort and encourage. God has given the prophet the ability to speak in a 'learned' manner, offering support and wisdom. He has been given this for the very specific purpose of speaking 'a word in season to him who is weary'. 'Morning by morning' God addresses the prophet – morning by morning the prophet prays to God, renewing his relationship with him, entering further into the covenant of love with him and, through this relationship, being able to hear the words that God wishes to speak to him. The emphasis is on regular conversation, regular listening – the prophet is awakened physically so that he can be awakened mentally, to enable him to 'hear as the learned'. Because of the depth of the relationship, and the trust the writer has in God, he can endure all sorts of suffering. We are reminded of the suffering of Christ in the details of the beatings on the back and face, and the shame of being spat upon. To have one's beard pulled out was, in those times, one of the worst humiliations that a man could suffer, yet the writer bears all this willingly – he gives his back and cheeks to his tormentors. Only one with a great trust in God would be able to serve as courageously as this. This section of Isaiah is often called the Second Servant Song. One of four poems focused on the figure of the 'servant of the Lord' found in the book of the prophet Isaiah, these poems could be the expression of the prophet himself, or of the ideal type of disciple, or of the people of Israel as a whole, who were probably in exile in Mesopotamia at that time. It is seen by many as a prophecy concerning the life and death of Christ, who accepts the cost of humanity willingly, aided by the strength and depth of his relationship with God. God is not the one who punishes here, but the one who suffers alongside his servant as he pours out his love for his people.

The power of regular, close contact with God through prayer is given great weight in this passage. It is through daily prayer – morning by morning – that the servant receives the wisdom and strength he needs to offer himself as a sacrifice for his people. It is through listening for God's word that he is given the words to speak that will serve as a comfort for those who are suffering. Very often we are quicker to speak than we are to listen – this passage reminds us that in order to have the wisdom to speak, we must first hear what is being said. Rather than bombarding God with a relentless list of requests for aid, even though these may not be made solely for ourselves but for others as well, we should cultivate times when we are prepared to sit and bear the silence, waiting in the presence of God. We may feel we hear little, but our willingness will not go unrewarded. So too in our relationship with others – listening is a greatly underrated skill, and generally to be preferred to that of speaking. Only when we have truly listened will the words we say be able to offer true comfort to the weary.

EXERCISE

Try to speak as little as possible for this day, or at least for part of the day. Instead, turn your attention to the words of others, listening closely to what they are saying, hearing their actual words without putting your own interpretation upon them. Try to be open to their meaning, and what it offers. If you are required to speak, pause and pray, even if it is for just a moment, before you do so. Allow yourself time to orient yourself before God, to open your ears to hear what he speaks, so that with the 'ear to hear' of 'the learned' you may speak with the 'tongue of the learned' – that is, one with compassion and love.

Walking in faith
LUKE 1.39–45

> At that time Mary got ready and hurried to a town in the hill country of Judea, where she entered Zechariah's home and greeted Elizabeth. When Elizabeth heard Mary's greeting, the baby leaped in her womb, and Elizabeth was filled with the Holy Spirit. In a loud voice she exclaimed: 'Blessed are you among women, and blessed is the child you will bear! But why am I so favoured, that the mother of my Lord should come to me? As soon as the sound of your greeting reached my ears, the baby in my womb leaped for joy. Blessed is she who has believed that the Lord would fulfil his promises to her!'

At first this seems to be an ordinary story about two ordinary women who are expecting babies. They are cousins, so it is only natural that one should journey to visit the other. Presumably they lived some distance apart, as it seems that Elizabeth did not know that Mary was pregnant. Elizabeth is delighted for her cousin's sake, and cries out with joy. But what she cries out gives the lie to the idea that this is just an ordinary event, and what we know reinforces this. For Mary and Elizabeth are not ordinary women – Elizabeth is well past the age of child bearing, and had long given up hope of ever becoming a mother. She may not even know that Zechariah was told of the birth of their son by an angel, because his disbelief caused him to be struck dumb. She is simply perplexed but delighted. But if Elizabeth is too old, Mary is too young – worse, she is not married. In Old Testament times, to be an unmarried mother was a great scandal, and Elizabeth, on seeing the condition of her cousin, affianced certainly, but not yet married, should by rights have been terribly shocked. According to the custom of the times, she should have spurned Mary, refusing to allow her to enter her home, and sent her away in disgrace. But as soon as she sees her, Elizabeth's unborn child leaps within her, and Elizabeth herself is 'filled with the Holy Spirit'. She ignores the conventions, puts aside all traditions of propriety, and welcomes Mary's arrival with joy and delight. Perhaps because Elizabeth herself has been on the receiving end of something totally unexpected, something wonderful and miraculous, she is prepared to accept this possibility in others. Perhaps the strange nature of the events that have happened to her have opened her mind to different ways of being, and she is better able to work with her intuition and her sense of the rightness of things, rather than simply working with the status quo. So too, when we are faced with the unexpected or the new, the mildly unconventional or the truly different, can we approach events and people with open hearts and minds, listening for the truth within what they are saying, trusting in our inner voice to listen and discern the nature of what we are hearing. We can set aside all that we expect to hear, the way we believe we should react, and examine an event in a different way, alert to God's voice within the words of others, trusting in our instinctive judgement as to what is right and wrong.

EXERCISE

The baby 'leaped' in his mother's womb to indicate his joy at the arrival of Mary, the Messiah-bearer. Already John was performing his task of prophet, of signpost to the Saviour. Practise walking in a relaxed and open way. Do not allow your shoulders or back to tense up, or your legs to stiffen, but walk slowly and mindfully for at least 15 minutes. Take time to observe how it feels to walk, the muscles you are using; notice if they seem tense at all or if you experience any discomfort. Do not worry about this, simply observe it and allow it to be, for now. Keep your shoulders down and relaxed, and walk with your head up, looking forward. Walk at a gentle pace, aware of your feet as they come into contact with the ground, feeling the air as it moves against your body. Be open to your physical reactions to the environment, and allow yourself to feel whatever it is you feel without judgement or expectation of a particular sensation. You might wish to pray on an in breath 'The Lord will fulfil' and on the out breath 'His promises to me'.

Hear then act
MARK 7.31–37

Then he returned from the region of Tyre, and went by way of Sidon towards the Sea of Galilee, in the region of the Decapolis. They brought to him a deaf man who had an impediment in his speech; and they begged him to lay his hand on him. He took him aside in private, away from the crowd, and put his fingers into his ears, and he spat and touched his tongue. Then looking up to heaven, he sighed and said to him, 'Ephphatha', that is, 'Be opened.' And immediately his ears were opened, his tongue was released, and he spoke plainly. Then Jesus ordered them to tell no one; but the more he ordered them, the more zealously they proclaimed it. They were astounded beyond measure, saying, 'He has done everything well; he even makes the deaf to hear and the mute to speak.'

It is hard to imagine how great the joy must have been among the community of Sidon when the man born deaf, unable to speak, can suddenly communicate with the rest of his people. The astonishment that must have rippled through the crowd who had brought the man to Jesus, probably as they had brought him to many other itinerant preachers and prophets before, in the hope of a cure. They might not have been very optimistic – after all, the others who had tried to cure him had failed – but perhaps they had heard that Jesus was different, that what he said would happen actually would. Anyway, what could they lose? And so Jesus opened the ears of the deaf man so that he could hear, and opened his mouth so that he could speak. Once more the man could play his proper role in his community, enjoying the privileges of communication, sharing the company of others. But Jesus does more than simply relieve the physical symptoms of deafness and blindness – and he does it for many more people than simply one person in an obscure settlement near the Sea of Galilee. He opens the eyes and ears of our hearts and minds so that we can hear and see the signs of his kingdom coming among us, and so that we can share the news of these signs with others. For there is a step that comes after hearing, which is to act upon that which we have heard. We can listen patiently for God's word, we can hear his call to us to act among his people with compassion and kindness, but if we fail to carry out that command, it is as if we have not heard at all. Christians are not people who hear the transforming message of Christ's sacrifice then spend the rest of their lives discussing it, or maybe planning how this transformation might occur – that is a trap into which it is all too easy to fall. Christians are those who have heard the message of the gospel and then share in its communication – they take the message into places where people are unable to hear it for themselves for there is no one to speak it to them. They take it to places where people are unable to speak because they have no voice, whether through poverty, oppression, ignorance, or places where the deaf and the mute still suffer. It is not enough to hear; we must act on what we have heard, and we must act now.

EXERCISE

Jesus healed the man who was deaf and dumb because his community brought him to Jesus and 'begged him' to heal him. Listen today to the voice of your community, and try to hear what it needs in terms of healing. Look around your place of work or leisure and notice its physical condition – is there something you could do to improve it? Take notice of the people who accompany you throughout your day – is there some way in which you could show them loving kindness or compassion? Take time to notice what is happening around you at every particular moment of the day, not allowing the moment to be obscured by future plans or past memories, but seeing what can be done, right now, to bring the kingdom closer.

Allowing the Spirit time
JOHN 8.2–11A

Early in the morning he came again to the temple. All the people came to him and he sat down and began to teach them. The scribes and the Pharisees brought a woman who had been caught in adultery; and making her stand before all of them, they said to him, 'Teacher, this woman was caught in the very act of committing adultery. Now in the law Moses commanded us to stone such women. Now what do you say?' They said this to test him, so that they might have some charge to bring against him. Jesus bent down and wrote with his finger on the ground. When they kept on questioning him, he straightened up and said to them, 'Let anyone among you who is without sin be the first to throw a stone at her.' And once again he bent down and wrote on the ground. When they heard it, they went away, one by one, beginning with the elders; and Jesus was left alone with the woman standing before him. Jesus straightened up and said to her, 'Woman, where are they? Has no one condemned you?' She said, 'No one, sir.' And Jesus said, 'Neither do I condemn you.'

Jesus knows he is being tested, he knows the scribes and the Pharisees are looking to bring charges against him. Some part of him must also have known that whatever answer he gave to the question they put before him, it would be twisted and corrupted until it met the purposes of those who plotted to destroy him. However, he must also have been very much aware that the life of a woman depended upon his answer. But it seems there is no correct answer, for adultery is condemned by the law and the prophets, but death by stoning is a savage and barbarous act that is quite against the peace-filled teaching of the kingdom-bringer. But Jesus refuses even to play their games. He refuses to be drawn into making a quick, on-the-spot answer, one that has not been properly thought out or reflected upon. Instead he pauses, and reflects in silence, drawing upon the ground while he turns the problem over in his mind. He ignores the obvious impatience of his questioners, preferring instead to seek wisdom in a time of silent thought. It is this determination not to be hurried into an answer, not to be rushed into following the crowd, coerced into responding as he knows he is being pressured to do, that is so vital. For it is in this space that the answer which Jesus needs arrives. It is in this space, this pause, this holding time, that the resolve not to follow the crowd or deliver the expected answer, develops. It is in this liminal space

31

that Jesus discerns that just because a thing has always been done in the past, does not mean it has to be done in the present. 'We always do it this way', with its emphasis on conforming to the established pattern, its harking back to the past, can often shut the door to new ways of thinking and behaving.

So too, when we feel pressured to give an immediate answer, or rushed into agreeing to something instantly, do we need to find the courage and strength to pause for a while and reflect. We need to make time to listen to our inner voice, the still small voice that is the voice of God, rather than give in to the clamour of the crowd which we hear calling for a consensus, holding to tradition, refusing to acknowledge the possibility of alternatives. Maybe in the moment of stillness, in our prayers for wisdom and insight, we too will find a new way, a way that honours instead of destroys, that brings new life instead of taking it away; a way that is unlike the old way but brings instead a different approach, one that is healing and grace filled, to a problem.

EXERCISE

It is very easy when we feel under pressure to make instant decisions. Sometimes the anxiety involved in reflecting on alternatives, the difficulty of trying to discern the right path, becomes too great and instead we choose the easy option, the one that is well tried and tested, the one that fits in with the wishes of the crowd. If you feel this happening to you today, try to take a three-minute breathing space before you make a decision. Pause and reflect – maybe even doodle or draw, just as Jesus did – allowing the Holy Spirit to work within you and lead you to a good decision.

SMELL

Finding peace in troubled times
JONAH 1.1–4, 15–17, 2.1–2A, 7–9

Now the word of the Lord came to Jonah son of Amittai, saying, 'Go at once to Nineveh, that great city, and cry out against it; for their wickedness has come up before me.' But Jonah set out to flee to Tarshish from the presence of the Lord. He went down to Joppa and found a ship going to Tarshish; so he paid his fare and went on board, to go with them to Tarshish, away from the presence of the Lord.
But the Lord hurled a great wind upon the sea, and such a mighty storm came upon the sea that the ship threatened to break up …

So they picked Jonah up and threw him into the sea; and the sea ceased from its raging. Then the men feared the Lord even more, and they offered a sacrifice to the Lord and made vows.

But the Lord provided a large fish to swallow up Jonah; and Jonah was in the belly of the fish for three days and three nights …

Then Jonah prayed to the Lord his God from the belly of the fish, saying …

'As my life was ebbing away,
I remembered the Lord;
and my prayer came to you,
into your holy temple.
Those who worship vain idols
forsake their true loyalty.

33

> *But I with the voice of thanksgiving*
> *will sacrifice to you;*
> *what I have vowed I will pay.*
> *Deliverance belongs to the Lord!'*

It is a familiar situation, with Jonah as with all of us. Jonah has an occupation – he is a prophet, one of those people set aside to bring the word of God to the community. He is charged with enthusing, encouraging, reminding and exhorting the people to remain in a strong relationship with God, and it is probable that he thoroughly enjoyed the position of privilege within the community which this role placed him in. However, Jonah is also responsible for transmitting God's words of reprimand and remonstration, which in turn would make him deeply unpopular with the people to whom he is communicating this sort of message. Unsurprisingly, Jonah is unwilling to engage with God's message, and instead runs away from what he perceives to be a situation that is potentially not only stressful, but even dangerous. God, however, has not finished with Jonah, and arranges matters in such a way that Jonah's attempt to escape his responsibilities endangers not only himself but others around him. Thrown into the sea, trapped for three days in the belly of a fish, among the stinking remains of the fish's previous meals, in the dark, stuffy atmosphere of a confined space, Jonah finally has to face up to the consequences of his actions. His response is not to mourn or to grieve at his captivity, nor less to rail in anger against the God who acted against him in such a draconian way. It is instead to raise his voice in a song of praise and thanksgiving. In this hymn of gratitude, Jonah responds as if he had already been rescued, so sure is he that his prayer will be answered. He vows to carry out God's commands and not to seek to flee from them any longer, because 'deliverance belongs to the Lord'.

Our unwillingness to face situations that we perceive to be potentially difficult and stressful is not unnatural – it is entirely normal to wish to avoid stress and unhappiness. However, it can be the case that the worry and anxiety over a prospective course of events can be even more difficult and stressful than the event itself. In effect, we have already lived out many times the worst possible scenarios, leaving us exhausted and less able to cope with the reality when it finally arrives. All lives contain unhappy events and situations, but these are inevitably made worse by living them in our imagination before they occur, looking forward to them with dread, comparing them to past difficulties, and imagining the outcome will be the same. Far better to accept a situation free from assumptions about the way it will play out, confident that we are in God's hands and therefore our deliverance belongs to him.

EXERCISE

When we are in difficult or challenging situations, it is very easy to feel as if these situations will last for ever. Jonah, as he sat in the belly of the whale in total darkness and surrounded by the terrible stench of rotting fish, must have had times of doubt as to whether he would ever breathe fresh air or see green fields and blue skies again. But he determinedly put aside these dark fears and focused on the positive; on his faith in a loving God who held Jonah in the palm of his hand, sheltering and protecting him.

Next time you are faced with a situation that seems to be beyond your control, or one that you cannot see ever ending or even improving, try using the breathing space or the body scan to gain some distance from your situation. Remember that in these practices the opportunity is given to observe feelings and emotions that threaten to overwhelm you in a way that gives you some distance from them, so that you can see them more clearly for what they are.

Find a quiet space where you can be still and comfortable. This can be sitting or lying, but it should be somewhere you can be still for a sustained period of time. Settle yourself so that you will remain alert and aware, and slow your breathing, gradually becoming aware of your physical surroundings – where your body touches your chair or the surface on which you are lying, how you feel within your clothes.

Beginning with your toes, try to discern any sensation or feeling in them. Don't worry if you feel nothing, sometimes this comes with continued practice of the body scan. If you feel discomfort in your toes, notice this. Try not to become involved in analysing the sensation or worrying about it; simply notice it without judging, allowing it to be what it is. Deepen your breathing, becoming aware of your breath flowing throughout your entire body, filling every blood cell with oxygen, sustaining life.

Gradually move your attention from your toes to your feet, then to the lower and upper parts of your legs. Steadily and slowly, focus on each part of your body in turn, resting your attention on it for 10 or 20 seconds, without deliberately counting the time, simply pausing long enough to register the sensations that you feel. If you feel tension or pain, breathe into them, exploring the feeling, allowing your mind to register the feeling without judging it, simply noticing it, before moving on.

Don't worry if your mind wanders – it probably will. When it does, simply bring it back to the task in hand, the task of the present, and continue your journey round your body.

After you have scanned your whole body, continue breathing in silence, aware of your body as a whole, loved by God, part of the unique individual that he formed for his loving purpose. You may wish to pray the first verses of Jonah's prayer, breathing in acceptance of a difficult situation, and breathing out God's spirit upon it:

> *I called to the Lord out of my distress,*
> *and he answered me;*
> *out of the belly of Sheol I cried,*
> *and you heard my voice.*
>
> Jonah 2.2b

Gaining distance
PSALM 115.1–13

Not to us, O Lord, not to us, but to your name give glory,
for the sake of your steadfast love and your faithfulness.
Why should the nations say,
'Where is their God?'

Our God is in the heavens;
he does whatever he pleases.
Their idols are silver and gold,
the work of human hands.
They have mouths, but do not speak;
eyes, but do not see.
They have ears, but do not hear;
noses, but do not smell.
They have hands, but do not feel;
feet, but do not walk;
they make no sound in their throats.
Those who make them are like them;
so are all who trust in them.

O Israel, trust in the Lord!
He is their help and their shield.
O house of Aaron, trust in the Lord!
He is their help and their shield.
You who fear the Lord, trust in the Lord!
He is their help and their shield.

The Lord has been mindful of us; he will bless us;
he will bless the house of Israel;
he will bless the house of Aaron;
he will bless those who fear the Lord,
both small and great.

It is not known precisely when this psalm was written, or who wrote it, but it is believed that it was written after the children of Israel had returned to their country from a place of exile after defeat in battle. Weary with struggle, they were trying to rebuild their temple and re-establish their worship practice, but were besieged on all sides by the taunts of those who followed the old ways, and challenged them to deliver evidence of the goodness of their God. Besides the visible nature of the idols, what could the children of Israel offer? The psalmist turns their taunts back upon his antagonists, pointing out that despite the great material value of their idols, they can, in fact, affect nothing. These figures of silver and gold were made by the people themselves, as opposed to being the creator of all living things. Again, these figures are unable to speak, to lead the people in the ways of truth and righteousness; they cannot hear the prayers that are spoken by the people and therefore cannot respond to them. They cannot be united in praise and worship and smell the incense of prayers that are offered to them. Only God can do all this; only with God can a relationship be formed that transforms those who enter into the covenant of love offered by an endlessly loving God. Today, our idols have different characteristics – they are not figures made of precious metals, but the metals themselves, as we chase after wealth and material goods. We seek power, fame, influence, putting these things before God and his kingdom. But these are all empty, worthless achievements that cannot offer us the help or support or love that we need to thrive as human beings. God, however, is 'mindful of us' and 'will bless us'; to him we can turn in times of trouble, confident that in him we will always find shelter. In him we will find the strength to meet the demands of the day, and through him we will gain our place in this world and the next, careful always to give God the glory; never seeking that glory for ourselves but offering it, in clouds of prayer, to the one from whom it came.

Our sense of smell is located in the olfactory bulb which is part of the brain's limbic system – an area that deals with our emotions and is strongly linked to our memories. The delight of our sense of smell is that it can call up memories and powerful associations. Newly mown grass can produce strong memories of childhood, for example, or a scent associated with a particular event can give us instant reminders of that occasion.

The danger of this is that we can be manipulated by our sense of smell into believing an event or a happening has to occur in the same way as it has in the past. The perfume industry makes good use of the emotive nature of our sense of smell to manipulate our emotions; we must take care that our awareness of situations is not hijacked by our emotions, that we do not make an instant fearful response on the basis of a past memory. Instead we can choose to observe those emotions without reacting to them, leaving us space to reflect on what is actually happening and take action.

EXERCISE

Next time you smell something that triggers an immediate emotional response, take time to notice that response and how it affects you. It could be a good feeling, such as the smell of freshly ground coffee reminding you of happy occasions drinking coffee with friends, or the smell of toast taking you back to childhood teatimes. It could be unpleasant – the smell of disinfectant bringing back memories of hospital visits, or lilies being a reminder of funerals. What is important is that you notice both the smell and the memory attached to it, without becoming involved in that memory — but simply being aware of it. In this way, a distance can be gained between an emotion and a reaction to an event. This in turn will provide the space that we need for dealing with the event.

Prayer rewarded
LUKE 1.5–20, 57, 62–64

In the time of Herod king of Judea there was a priest named Zechariah, who belonged to the priestly division of Abijah; his wife Elizabeth was also a descendant of Aaron. Both of them were righteous in the sight of God, observing all the Lord's commands and decrees blamelessly. But they were childless because Elizabeth was not able to conceive, and they were both very old.

Once when Zechariah's division was on duty and he was serving as priest before God, he was chosen by lot, according to the custom of the priesthood, to go into the temple of the Lord and burn incense. And when the time for the burning of incense came, all the assembled worshippers were praying outside.

Then an angel of the Lord appeared to him, standing at the right side of the altar of incense. When Zechariah saw him, he was startled and was gripped with fear. But the angel said to him: 'Do not be afraid, Zechariah; your prayer has been heard. Your wife Elizabeth will bear you a son, and you are to call him John. He will be a joy and delight to you, and many will rejoice because of his birth, for he will be great in the sight of the Lord. He is never to take wine or other fermented drink, and he will be filled with the Holy Spirit even before he is born. He will bring back many of the people of Israel to the Lord their God. And he will go on before the Lord, in the spirit and power of Elijah,

*to turn the hearts of the parents to their children and the
disobedient to the wisdom of the righteous – to make ready
a people prepared for the Lord.'*

*Zechariah asked the angel, 'How can I be sure of this? I
am an old man and my wife is well on in years.'*

*The angel said to him, 'I am Gabriel. I stand in the
presence of God, and I have been sent to speak to you and
to tell you this good news. And now you will be silent and
not able to speak until the day this happens, because you
did not believe my words, which will come true at their
appointed time' …*

*When it was time for Elizabeth to have her baby, she
gave birth to a son.*

*Then they made signs to his father, to find out what he
would like to name the child. He asked for a writing tablet,
and to everyone's astonishment he wrote, 'His name is John.'
Immediately his mouth was opened and his tongue set free,
and he began to speak, praising God.*

Zechariah and his wife Elizabeth are examples of that unfortunate
group of people who, through no fault of their own, are visited
by sadness during their lives. That they were good people, and
undeserving of their lot, is made very clear by Luke as he tells
their tale – they were 'righteous in the sight of God'. But instead
of the fortune and happiness that we sometimes feel should
be the only natural consequence of behaving 'blamelessly' for
many years, they were condemned to a life of childlessness.
Always a tragedy for anyone who longs for a child, but in the
time of Zechariah and Elizabeth the lack of an heir was close
to disaster. When the couple grew old, there would be no one
to support them in a civilization that did not have a public
welfare system; if Zechariah died young, Elizabeth would be
destitute without a relative to look after her. In addition to this,
misfortune of such kinds was often looked on by others as a
punishment sent by God for an individual's misdeeds – how

Zechariah must have suffered from the suspicion of his fellow priests that his life was not as free from sin as it really was, and that he was in fact hiding some mortal fault from the rest of the world! He must have felt greatly relieved when finally his name was chosen by lot to be one of those who burnt incense at the altar of the Lord in the great temple – perhaps he might have felt finally vindicated that God's choice had fallen upon him, perhaps that this privilege might indicate to his priestly companions that he had not been abandoned by God after all. To be chosen for this task was indeed a fortunate thing: it has been calculated that since every direct descendant of Aaron was a priest, there might perhaps have been as many as 20,000 priests serving in the temple. For practical purposes they were divided into sections of 1,000 each, and every section served in the temple for two weeks in the year. The tasks of these priests were allocated by lot – to be chosen was possibly the pinnacle of any priest's life. And here was Zechariah, at last serving in the temple.

But the incidents of the day did not end there for Zechariah, for, when he entered the inner sanctum of the temple, he saw an angel to one side of the altar. The angel spoke to him and told him that the days of childlessness were over for him and his wife as, despite their great age, God had decided that they were to have a son. This child would not only be a 'joy and delight' to them, but he would also be 'great in the sight of the Lord' – what parent could wish for more? Finally, after years of blameless living and conscientious service, the couple were to receive their reward!

Perhaps it was because Zechariah had spent so many years building up his defences against the suspicions of his fellow priests as to the reason for his childlessness, perhaps it was because although he 'served all the Lord's commandments and regulations blamelessly' but without joy or delight, perhaps he had become so embittered by his failure to produce an heir that he could not see beyond this fact to the other blessings in his life, but Zechariah does not accept the message of the angel. Instead he argues with him, telling the angel that this is not how things work in this world, that elderly couples do not have their longings fulfilled in such a complete and wonderful fashion. Zechariah's mind is so full of memories and assumptions from past experiences that he cannot hear the truth of what the angel is saying but instead overlays it with what he thinks the angel is saying.

This is not how human beings should interact with God, and Zechariah is reprimanded and made mute until the birth of the boy, John. But neither is this how human beings should react to each other. Sometimes we allow our thoughts to take over our conscious mind without being aware that this is happening. When new events occur, we try to put them in categories of events that have happened before, rather than being open to them as new experiences, with new possibilities and outcomes. Zechariah's refusal to accept the news of the angel means that but for the grace of God he would have missed out on the miracle of fatherhood. Pushed into attitudes of mind and behaviour by previous experiences, he lacks the openness and flexibility of mind to appreciate new opportunities. So too do we allow memories of past events to influence our reactions to current happenings, with the possibility that we misjudge them, to our loss.

EXERCISE

Try to look at each event and experience of the day with new eyes. Try to think and behave and react to the tasks and interactions of the day as if it were the first time they had happened. This won't be easy, and at times will not be appropriate as there are occasions when our experience is precious and our skills honed to a high degree of effectiveness. But we can, even then, try to look at our thoughts and reactions from a distance, instead of inhabiting them. We can refuse to allow preconceptions and prejudices to influence our thoughts and behaviour, and instead remain open to the event itself and the way it unfolds in this particular way, on this particular day.

One small change
JOHN 2.13–22

> *The Passover of the Jews was near, and Jesus went up to Jerusalem. In the temple he found people selling cattle, sheep, and doves, and the money-changers seated at their tables. Making a whip of cords, he drove all of them out of the temple, both the sheep and the cattle. He also poured out the coins of the money-changers and overturned their tables. He told those who were selling the doves, 'Take these things out of here! Stop making my Father's house a market-place!' His disciples remembered that it was written, 'Zeal for your house will consume me.' The Jews then said to him, 'What sign can you show us for doing this?' Jesus answered them, 'Destroy this temple, and in three days I will raise it up.' The Jews then said, 'This temple has been under construction for forty-six years, and will you raise it up in three days?' But he was speaking of the temple of his body. After he was raised from the dead, his disciples remembered that he had said this; and they believed the scripture and the word that Jesus had spoken.*

When Jesus entered the temple in Jerusalem just before the time of the Passover, that great festival of the Jewish faith, it is probable that he was seeking, as was his custom, a quiet place to pray. Throughout the Gospels are references to Jesus' frequent times of prayer, particularly necessary before or after events of great significance or importance. At those times, Jesus would go apart from his disciples and from the people who besieged him with their requests for help and healing, and seek healing for himself in the reconnection of his heart and mind with God, reaffirming their living relationship. Places of wilderness are often mentioned, as are excursions in a boat on the Sea of Galilee, but there were no such opportunities in the city, so he was forced to make the temple his destination. And this was a sound decision, for it was in the temple that people prayed, and made their sacrifices to God for their sins. But it was the time of the Passover, and the temple was busy. Historians have estimated that the population of Jerusalem swelled from around 50,000–60,000 to nearly one million during the festival, and all of these people needed to visit the temple during their stay. They would not, of course, have entered the inner sanctum, which was reserved only for the priests, but they would certainly have been in the outer precincts. Here they would be found buying animals for the ritual sacrifice – goats or doves – and changing money into Tyrian silver for the temple tax. Here too would be carried out the ritual slaughter of the animals and, with so many thousands of pilgrims needing to do this, the place would have become like an abattoir, with the noise of frightened animals, and the sickening smell of blood and dirt pervading the entire set of buildings like a miasma of distress. It is not, therefore, surprising that Jesus lost his temper, and drove everyone from the area. What had been originally set down in the Torah as an aid to prayer, a way of reaffirming the covenant between God and his people, had degenerated into a barrier between the people and God, a barrier of noise and smell, confusion and argument.

Our habits too can become like this – preferences, routines and rituals that were originally helpful and productive can cease to become so over the years as circumstances and personalities change and develop. We must be mindful of those actions we perform that we take for granted are beneficial to our situation, rather than detrimental to it, that they promote growth and wholeness rather than perpetuate insecurity and anxiety.

EXERCISE

Try today to change one thing that you regularly do. This can be small, such as changing the chair you usually sit in, or rather more demanding, such as changing the route of a journey you make regularly, or the pattern of your morning or evening. Notice the feelings that are generated by your action – are you discomforted by what happens, is the disruption a pleasant surprise or a time-consuming difficulty? Being jolted out of the ruts that we have made for ourselves will encourage us to live in the moment as we re-engage with an activity that had become such a habit it wasn't noticed. Changing small things about our lives might encourage and enable us to change bigger, more damaging habits – a dependence on cigarettes or alcohol, a shopping or gambling inclination. Aware of the moment, we might be able to focus on the things we habitually say or think about ourselves or others – things that are damaging and untrue, but that have become part of our thinking over time.

Breathing in
MATTHEW 6.25–34

'Therefore I tell you, do not worry about your life, what you will eat or drink; or about your body, what you will wear. Is not life more important than food, and the body more than clothes? Look at the birds of the air; they do not sow or reap or store away in barns, and yet your heavenly Father feeds them. Are you not much more valuable than they? Can any one of you by worrying add a single hour to your life?

'And why do you worry about clothes? See how the flowers of the field grow. They do not labour or spin. Yet I tell you that not even Solomon in all his splendour was dressed like one of these. If that is how God clothes the grass

of the field, which is here today and tomorrow is thrown into the fire, will he not much more clothe you – you of little faith? So do not worry, saying, "What shall we eat?" or "What shall we drink?" or "What shall we wear?" For the pagans run after all these things, and your heavenly Father knows that you need them. But seek first his kingdom and his righteousness, and all these things will be given to you as well. Therefore do not worry about tomorrow, for tomorrow will worry about itself. Each day has enough trouble of its own.'

This passage might almost be called the seminal gospel on mindfulness. With great love and tender compassion, Jesus tells his followers that they have got their priorities all wrong. Preoccupied with anxieties about the future and fretful thoughts about what this future will bring, they are missing not only some of the greatest gifts that God's creation can offer, but they are wasting their time, energy and emotions on things that are simply not as important as they think they are. One of the rules of successful business is always to 'keep the main thing, the main thing', and this rule extends outwards not only to our everyday lives but inwards to our spiritual lives. Time spent on agitating about future events, seeing if they might fit into a pattern from the past, and so prove predictable in their outcome, is time taken away from the vital task of seeking the 'kingdom [of God] and his righteousness', the true focus for our attentions. Jesus assures us that just like the smallest part of creation, we are being held in God's loving care. We are constantly in his mind, our every action of great importance to him. This reassurance should give us the courage we need to let go of our concerns for the future, and even our anxious self-querying about the state of our emotions and why they are such as they are. Too often, the greatest stress comes from our self-analysis about our state of mind. Distressed at our unhappiness or our stress, dissatisfied with what we perceive to be the enormous gap between how we feel and how we would like to feel, how we think we should feel, we turn our gaze destructively inwards, fermenting plans to bridge this gap. Safe in the hands of God, we can let go of our thoughts and worries, giving them no more energy than that required simply to observe them objectively. It is then that we will find the time and the space to reflect on the tasks we are being given for this day, this moment, and discover the strength to accomplish those tasks to the glory of God, putting the claims of his kingdom first in our lives.

EXERCISE

If you can, buy some strongly scented flowers – lilies, roses, gardenia, phlox and lily of the valley are all wonderfully fragrant. Or you can find flowers growing wild, in the hedgerows or in parks – honeysuckle, rambling roses, lilac or lavender. If these options are not available, flower-scented soaps or candles will be fine. Place the flowers where their scent will reach you, and carry out either a body scan or a three-minute breathing space, depending on how much time you have. During your reflection, take some time to focus on the scents that are filling your nose, breathing deeply, aware of the slightest scent sensation. You might want to end your meditation by breathing in the words of Jesus: 'seek first his kingdom and his righteousness' or 'do not worry about tomorrow, for tomorrow will worry about itself'.

SIGHT

Leaving burdens behind
GENESIS 19.15–17, 24–26

When morning dawned, the angels urged Lot, saying, 'Get up, take your wife and your two daughters who are here, or else you will be consumed in the punishment of the city.' But he lingered; so the men seized him and his wife and his two daughters by the hand, the Lord being merciful to him, and they brought him out and left him outside the city. When they had brought them outside, they said, 'Flee for your life; do not look back or stop anywhere in the Plain; flee to the hills, or else you will be consumed' …

Then the Lord rained on Sodom and Gomorrah sulphur and fire from the Lord out of heaven; and he overthrew those cities, and all the Plain, and all the inhabitants of the cities, and what grew on the ground. But Lot's wife, behind him, looked back, and she became a pillar of salt.

Lot was one of the faithful who had travelled with Abraham from Ur to Canaan. But when Abraham unselfishly offered him the first choice of land to settle in, Lot chose the easy way, the lush and fertile area, and so came to Sodom. Two angels disguised as visitors meet Lot as he sits at the city gate, the place where the leaders of the town traditionally met to sort out financial and legal matters. Clearly Lot has been completely assimilated into the lifestyle of Sodom – it would not be surprising if he had become caught up in their ways also. Perhaps this is why, when he and his family are offered a chance of escape, he finds it hard to leave everything behind him and just go. He lingers, caught up perhaps in the agony of the losses he is about to suffer.

49

Everything he has worked for, his material goods, his position in the city, his comfort, his security, is about to disappear. Even though the entire city was depraved and corrupt – for in what other sort of city would the entire male population turn out to assault strangers? – Lot had become accustomed to its ways and was finding it hard to leave behind.

This reluctance is witnessed in even stronger terms in Lot's wife. This woman, whose name we do not even know, is so regretful that despite the strongest exhortations she cannot resist the impulse to turn back to look on the city she is leaving behind. The verb in Hebrew that is translated by 'looked back' signifies 'intense gaze'. The pull of the past is too strong for her; she cannot turn and face the future because she is preoccupied with what has gone before, and this destroys her.

This passage is a stark warning against the dangers of becoming compromised by the worldly and secular society in which we live. Lot has spent too long among the people of Sodom, too little time reminding himself of his status as a child of God, and he is heavily influenced by the lifestyle and values of those around him. His regrets nearly cost him his life; they cost Lot's wife hers. But this is more than a simple diatribe against living 'with the enemy'. In a subtler way it is a warning against being so preoccupied with what has gone before that we cannot see the avenues of possibility that are opening up in front of us. Lot and his wife have been saved from death by angels; surely they can trust that they will not be abandoned by God? But Lot's wife cannot see this and needs to look back at what she has lost, fearing that the future will not be as good as the past – damaged and destructive as that past was. We must be aware of looking constantly to the past, of missing the possibilities of a new and changed future because we are full of regrets for what is behind us, even if our past is not a particularly happy place, simply a familiar one. 'Looking back' will often cause us to stumble, especially if we allow what is behind us to influence our attitude to what is ahead.

EXERCISE

Imagine yourself in the company of Lot and his family, stumbling anxiously across the plain to a place of safety. Behind you lies certain death – your home city in ruins, burning with the hottest fires; your possessions, your fine furniture, precious treasures, costly objects, are melting and running into one another, so great is the heat of the flames that devour them. Your past life is over, a new one lies ahead, full of uncertainty and danger but also under the sure protection and shelter of God. Now, picture instead of material goods some of those habits of thought and behaviour that you know are dangerous and damaging but still cling on to, perhaps because they have become a habit, perhaps because they bring you some comfort, even though you know they are doing you harm. These habits could be a dependence on addictive substances, overeating, shopping, or they could be less easily identifiable – a tendency to anxiety, a habit of pessimism. They could be concerns about worldly wealth or status, a willingness to compromise values and principles for the purposes of success or power. Allow the flames to burn these also, destroying their ability to control your life or influence the way you make decisions. Then, without looking back, walk on, free from burdens.

The world in a grain of sand
ISAIAH 42.5–9

> *Thus says God, the Lord,*
> *who created the heavens and stretched them out,*
> *who spread out the earth and what comes from it,*
> *who gives breath to the people upon it*
> *and spirit to those who walk in it:*
> *I am the Lord, I have called you in righteousness,*

51

I have taken you by the hand and kept you;
I have given you as a covenant to the people,
a light to the nations,
to open the eyes that are blind,
to bring out the prisoners from the dungeon,
from the prison those who sit in darkness.
I am the Lord, that is my name;
my glory I give to no other,
nor my praise to idols.
See, the former things have come to pass,
and new things I now declare;
before they spring forth,
I tell you of them.

In the Common Worship lectionary, used by many Anglican churches throughout the world, this passage is set for the Baptism of Christ. It is a passage full of wonder, and a reminder of the greatness of God's promises, brought to fruition in Jesus. Isaiah takes us right back to the beginning of creation, when there was nothing but darkness and chaos, out of which God brought the heavens and the earth and everything that comes from it. He reminds us of the glories of creation that surround us, the infinite wonders of nature that are paraded before our eyes every minute of every day, a day that follows on each previous day with the certainty of God's promises to us. Isaiah reminds us that we have been created by God, but that even more we have been given 'breath' by God – we have been filled with the breath of his Spirit and are his children. The image of the child is continued as Isaiah tells us that God has taken us by the hand and kept us safe, every one of us, and that we can rely upon him to continue to do so from the depths of his love, which has been given to us in the person of Christ. But this passage is not just a promise and a reassurance of God's continued care for each one of us, it is a commission as well. In this passage the call is not just for us to remember the God whose power and love created the heavens and earth, but for us to share that news with those we meet, to open the eyes of those around us who are blind to the love of God and help them to see, to release our communities from the darkness of ignorance and anxiety, of desperation and obsession, and show them a new way to live. We are called to be heralds of the 'new things' that will spring forth and, in doing so, enable their arrival. The passage is charged with energy and excitement, springing forth from that first great miracle of creation and blossoming into redemption and freedom for all people.

EXERCISE

To see a World in a Grain of Sand
And a Heaven in a Wild Flower
Hold Infinity in the palm of your hand
And Eternity in an hour

These words from the poem 'Auguries of Innocence' by the nineteenth-century poet William Blake remind us that the infinite love of our creator God surrounds us on every side. All things are witnesses to God's love, and it is our joy to take notice of them. We have a duty to move slowly and carefully through the world, giving value and glory to the love that surrounds us, evidenced both in the works of nature and in those people with whom we share our lives. Take some time today to study one natural object. It does not have to be very large or particularly special, or even very appealing, it simply has to exist, because that is what God made it for. Pick up the object, if you can, feel its texture, notice its smell, appreciate the great variety of colours and shapes that are held within its form. Remember that just as God's love extends to this tiny fragment of creation, so too does it reach out to every human being on the planet. How would you open the eyes of another to the wonders of this object? What words would you use to describe it to someone who had not seen it before?

Imagine yourself as held by God as you hold this object, sheltered and safe, every detail noticed and appreciated, redeemed by Christ's saving action and made perfect in his grace.

Rejoice!
MARK 13.34–37

'It is like a man going to a far country, who left his house and gave authority to his servants, and to each his work, and commanded the doorkeeper to watch. Watch therefore, for you do not know when the master of the house is coming – in the evening, at midnight, at the crowing of the rooster, or in the morning – lest, coming suddenly, he find you sleeping. And what I say to you, I say to all: Watch!'

Within the Christian year, the time of Advent is traditionally one of preparation for Christmas. However, this preparation extends far beyond the secular jobs of buying presents, preparing food and tidying the house for visitors. Christians have a far more significant task to carry out – to prepare our souls for the coming of the Lord at the end of time. This sounds very dramatic, but there is throughout the gospel a sense of urgency brought to us by Jesus' constant warnings and reminders that we should make ourselves ready for the coming of the kingdom. When that time will be, we do not know, but we should be ready for it, whenever it occurs. Fortunately for us, this time of repentance and preparation takes place just before the feast of Christmas, because through this we are reminded that our salvation is already assured through the action of Christ, who came to earth to redeem us from our sins.

So where does this leave the mindful Christian? Surely a

constant state of looking ahead to the future, making desperate preparations for an event about which we know very little and, in our sinful state, may have much to be anxious about, is not a mindful practice? In truth, the admonition to watch and wait does appear at first glance to sit uneasily with a focus of attention on the 'now', but this is to misunderstand – or perhaps only partly understand – the message of the Gospels. In the passage we look at today, the Son of Man is compared to someone going on a journey, who gives his household instructions as to how they are to behave in his absence. We do not know what this man is like as a householder, but we do know that Jesus left us at the time of his Ascension, promising to return at the end of time – that same loving Jesus who spent his life on earth healing, praying, teaching and caring for all people with a great compassion. So his return may not be something to be feared, as it is often interpreted, but something to be rejoiced at. This is especially the case if we have been faithful and honest in the way we have been living in the interim. Notice how the household workers in the passage are each given a specific task to do. This task is presumably within their skills and abilities, and should be carried out with care and integrity, otherwise the smooth running of the household will be disrupted and affairs will be disorganized and falling apart by the time the owner returns. Jesus does not say that the tasks are particularly difficult or demanding, simply that each person is given their own to fulfil faithfully, and surely that is what is being requested of us also? We are not asked to do more than we are able, we are not asked to be greater or more successful or even busier than we can manage, simply to do the best we can, as faithfully as we can, until Jesus returns, and we are gathered up together to be with him in eternity. Yes, we are told, we should be alert and awake, and we should certainly watch for signs of the coming kingdom. However, we also know that the kingdom is here among us, and some of the signs we are watching for are already present, in the words and actions of those who surround us, in the way we strive to fulfil our potential as people of God. Instead of looking to the future with great fear, constantly creating scenarios of unpleasantness from the depths of our imagination, we should be focusing on the 'now', and living the best way we can within it. Mindful Christians do not allow their memories of the past or their plans for the future to be anything more than what they are – moments in the past and possibilities for the future. They are not the present reality, which is now, and is designed by a loving God to be lived in as fully as possible.

EXERCISE

Try to spend part of this day simply rejoicing in the activities of the day itself. Try for as long a period of time as possible to move your mind from memories of the past to focusing on the present. Avoid looking to the future, making plans, imagining how events will work out, worrying about what might happen. Each time your mind drifts to either of these actions, notice what has made you concerned, but do not give it any energy; simply bring your thoughts gently back to the present. Accept your life for what it is, right now. The past is part of you and the future will be also, but for now, for a short time, don't waste the good that is surrounding you by worrying about the future – make your 'watching' count!

Cheerful actions
ROMANS 13.11–14

Besides this, you know what time it is, how it is now the moment for you to wake from sleep. For salvation is nearer to us now than when we became believers; the night is far gone, the day is near. Let us then lay aside the works of darkness and put on the armour of light; let us live honourably as in the day, not in revelling and drunkenness, not in debauchery and licentiousness, not in quarrelling and jealousy. Instead, put on the Lord Jesus Christ, and make no provision for the flesh, to gratify its desires.

The sense of urgency that we first noticed in Jesus calling us to watch and stay awake is continued in Paul's letters to the churches. It has been suggested that this urgency is caused by Paul's belief that the end time was very near, and would in fact happen during his own lifetime. It was his duty, therefore, to exhort his fellow Christians to prepare themselves for an imminent event; hence his extreme pressure for people to accept Christ into their lives before it was too late. But Paul kept this enthusiasm and sense of energy throughout his life, and his letter to the Romans was written possibly some 60 years after the death and resurrection of Christ. What drove him was his conviction that the life, death and resurrection of Jesus Christ had changed the whole world for ever; that because of Christ's saving action, people need no longer live in fear but in faith and hope. The question that concerned him was how he and his fellow Christians should live within the new relationship they now had with God and with one another, how their transformed relationship with a reality that contained all the fulfilled promises of God should be inhabited, not only by a different way of thinking, but by a different way of living, and how this way of life should look. For Paul, the life to be lived was one of faith, a faith in the loving purposes of God that it drove out all fear, all anxiety, and all concern for the future or regret for the past. The past has been redeemed and transformed by Christ's action on the cross, the future is not yet here – the present is all that we have to live in, and it is in the hands of a loving, faithful God. We no longer need to seek to dull our anxieties or fears through the drugs of addictive behaviour, we no longer need to cut off our constant worry for the future by immersing ourselves in mindless activities or deadening consumerism –

we can turn in faith and hope to God, and put ourselves in his loving hands.

Paul tells us that we know what the time is – it is not 'then' or 'will be' but 'now', the only moment in which we can act and in which we can truly engage with reality. We need to let go of our constant examination of the difference between our lives now and our lives as we would like them to be, we need to cease harking back to past events that we fear will shape our future, and instead see the moment as it really is, free from thoughts and anxieties that distort and corrupt. 'Seize the day' is not a phrase designed to encourage us to expend our energy and resources on empty activities, but to enable us to live fully in the present, a present transformed by God and our relationship with him, a present in which we can trust and in which we will find the kingdom of God.

EXERCISE

Choose one of the many routine activities that you will undertake today, and resolve to perform it as cheerfully as possible, delighting in the skills and abilities that you need to carry out the task and rejoicing in the fact that you are able to do it. Try to think of ways to make this task one that will bring nearer the kingdom of God – either through thought, word or action. Encourage those who surround you with kind words perhaps, pick up litter from the street you walk along, undertake a task for someone else, or simply put your whole heart into carrying out the action as best as you can.

Don't walk by the colour purple
LUKE 15.11–20

> *Then Jesus said, 'There was a man who had two sons. The younger of them said to his father, "Father, give me the share of the property that will belong to me." So he divided his property between them. A few days later the younger son gathered all he had and travelled to a distant country, and there he squandered his property in dissolute living. When he had spent everything, a severe famine took place throughout that country, and he began to be in need. So he went and hired himself out to one of the citizens of that country, who sent him to his fields to feed the pigs. He would gladly have filled himself with the pods that the pigs were eating; and no one gave him anything. But when he came to himself he said, "How many of my father's hired hands have bread enough and to spare, but here I am dying of hunger! I will get up and go to my father, and I will say to him, 'Father, I have sinned against heaven and before you; I am no longer worthy to be called your son; treat me like one of your hired hands.'" So he set off and went to his father. But while he was still far off, his father saw him and was filled with compassion; he ran and put his arms around him and kissed him.'*

The images in this story are very powerful, both the outward ones that can be seen by everyone, and the inward ones that are seen only by the eye of the mind. The story centres on realization, on coming to one's senses, and on repentance, a turning towards and a reconciliation.

There is no doubt that the young man is gravely in the wrong with his initial actions. To ask for one's inheritance before a parent has died is as good as wishing that person were already dead. It is an action that disregards human relationship and raises material concerns to a higher level than anything else.

It isn't surprising that the man squanders his money – anyone who can be as reckless as he is with the sensitivities and feelings of another human being might well be reckless in other ways too. It isn't until he is brought very low indeed, feeding pigs in fact – those animals counted as unclean by the Jewish people – that he comes to himself, as the translation puts it. He suddenly has a clear image in the eye of his mind of the most menial of his father's workforce, and he realizes what he had not noticed before: that they were in fact decently treated and well fed. The clearness of that vision leads him to a further realization – of the enormity of his past actions and a desire to put them right. He does not turn away from his present condition; rather, he turns towards something better, holding a picture in his imagination that he makes his goal.

And all this time his father has been keeping watch for him. It is easy to imagine the old man constantly scanning the horizon, hoping to see a familiar figure silhouetted against the distant landscape, straining his eyes whenever a stranger approaches in the hope that it is no stranger but his son. Finally, his heart's desire is granted and the father runs to meet his son, a dramatic and unusual occurrence, since to run would have damaged the dignity of the head of a large household, who would not normally run anywhere! Gone is the notion of a formal greeting or an official reception. There is no period of adjustment, when the father tries to make sure that his son realizes the extent of his crime and is truly sorry for it – forgiveness is instant and permanent. The beloved son is safe home once more.

So too does God eagerly seek us, whenever we turn away from him, whenever we change our priorities or adjust our values to those of the secular world. The image of his loving forgiveness remains in our mind's eye, ready when we turn back to it to become a reality. It is only when we stop believing that just because life is how it is, that is how it must remain, that we can become open to new possibilities and different futures. It is only when we turn again to God that we can see the potential that lies within each one of us as his redeemed children.

So too can we scan our own external and internal landscapes for signs of the kingdom, noticing each detail, seeking God in our surroundings. We can rejoice in the signs of God's love that surround us every day, delighting in the treasures he is offering us, feeding our souls with much needed food so that we do not go hungry.

EXERCISE

In her famous novel *The Color Purple*, Alice Walker writes about the feeling of connectedness with the whole created kingdom, and the glory of our surroundings:

> *But one day when I was sitting quiet and feeling like a motherless child, which I was, it come to me: that feeling of being part of everything, not separate at all. I knew that if I cut a tree, my arm would bleed. And I laughed and cried and I run all around the house. I knew just what it was. In fact, when it happen, you can't miss it … I think it pisses God off if you walk by the color purple in a field somewhere and don't notice it.*

> Alice Walker, *The Color Purple*, Harcourt
> Brace Jovanovich, 1982

Try today to notice everything that is a particular colour. It doesn't have to be purple, but it might be easier if you do choose an unusual colour or you might not make much progress with the rest of your day! Notice the different shades in which your colour appears, the different uses that are made of it. Pause by an object that is completely in your chosen colour and spend time just looking at it, absorbing its detail.

Finding aspects of beauty
MARK 10.46–52

> *They came to Jericho. As he and his disciples and a large crowd were leaving Jericho, Bartimaeus son of Timaeus, a blind beggar, was sitting by the roadside. When he heard that it was Jesus of Nazareth, he began to shout out and say, 'Jesus, Son of David, have mercy on me!' Many sternly ordered him to be quiet, but he cried out even more loudly, 'Son of David, have mercy on me!' Jesus stood still and said, 'Call him here.' And they called the blind man, saying to him, 'Take heart; get up, he is calling you.' So throwing off his cloak, he sprang up and came to Jesus. Then Jesus said to him, 'What do you want me to do for you?' The blind man said to him, 'My teacher, let me see again.' Jesus said to him, 'Go; your faith has made you well.' Immediately he regained his sight and followed him on the way.*

A blind man is healed. Someone who could not see is made to see again – another miracle is performed and Jesus can continue on his way. But what makes this miracle so special, one that cannot be swept up in one of those general statements that occur periodically throughout the Gospels: 'and [he] cured all who were sick' (Matthew 8.16) or he 'healed those who needed to be cured' (Luke 9.11)? The significance of this passage is that even before Blind Bartimaeus, beggar, becomes Bartimaeus, disciple, he demonstrates an ability to see something, despite his blindness, that even Jesus' disciples with their perfect vision have failed to notice. Bartimaeus does not need literally to see Jesus to recognize who he is – as he passes by, Jesus is hailed by him 'Jesus, Son of David, have mercy on me!' He uses those famous words, which later become a powerful prayer in themselves (see page 113 on the Jesus Prayer), and shouts them out, ignoring the attempts of those around him to silence him. Bartimaeus has recognized the truth of Jesus, and the truth must be proclaimed. And it is this recognition, this willingness to believe, this faith, that triggers his healing, as Jesus declares 'Go! Your faith has made you well!' There is a feeling that the curing of blindness is incidental, for Bartimaeus' declaration has brought him in reach of the salvation of Christ, just as in Matthew 9 the paralytic is first healed of his sins, and then cured of his paralysis. By recognizing Jesus as the Son of God, a new way of life is opened up to Bartimaeus and it is one that he chooses to take, as he does not remain in Jericho, his home town, but follows Jesus on the way.

The disciples did eventually recognize Jesus – they identified him in and through the things he did in their presence: teaching, healing, loving and forgiving. Christ is here today wherever we are right now, and wherever we next go on to. Christ will appear before us as we move about and talk and work with people. Let us make each moment a miracle of sight as we see Christ in the faces of those around us and celebrate the extraordinary within the everyday.

EXERCISE

Try to see aspects of Christ in the actions and words of those whom you spend this day with. Try to see them as Jesus would, with eyes of loving forgiveness and understanding. Try to see their words and actions clearly, for what they are, rather than clogged with the dust and dirt of previous encounters. Try to be objective about what you see and hear, to notice the words and actions themselves simply for what they are, and not to inflict interpretations on them which perhaps come from yourself, your memories and experiences, rather than what is actually being said and done.

If you are with a group or crowd of people, try to recognize the face of Christ in those who surround you. Pray for them, that they may be happy and healthy, that they may find peace, that they and those they love may spend their time in enjoyment of each other's company. Without staring, try to find aspects of beauty and love in each person you encounter, and pray that whatever good resides in their hearts will flourish and blossom in love.

TOUCH

Washing clean
2 KINGS 5.1–3, 9–14

Now Naaman, captain of the host of the king of Syria, was a great man with his master, and honourable, because by him the Lord had given deliverance unto Syria; he was also a mighty man in valour, but he was a leper.

And the Syrians had gone out by companies, and had brought away captive out of the land of Israel a little maid; and she waited on Naaman's wife.

And she said unto her mistress, Would God my lord were with the prophet that is in Samaria! for he would recover him of his leprosy …

So Naaman came with his horses and with his chariot, and stood at the door of the house of Elisha.

And Elisha sent a messenger unto him, saying, Go and wash in Jordan seven times, and thy flesh shall come again to thee, and thou shalt be clean.

But Naaman was wroth, and went away, and said, Behold, I thought, he will surely come out to me, and stand, and call on the name of the Lord his God, and strike his hand over the place, and recover the leper.

Are not Abana and Pharpar, rivers of Damascus, better than all the waters of Israel? may I not wash in them, and be clean? So he turned and went away in a rage.

And his servants came near, and spake unto him, and said, My father, if the prophet had bid thee do some great

> *thing, wouldest thou not have done it? How much rather then, when he saith to thee, Wash and be clean?*
>
> *Then went he down, and dipped himself seven times in Jordan, according to the saying of the man of God: and his flesh came again like unto the flesh of a little child, and he was clean.*

It might appear that Naaman had everything anyone could wish for – he was a powerful man, skilled at his job, possessing the confidence of those for whom he worked. He was married, he was wealthy, and he appeared to have few character flaws. All would have been well but for the fact that he was stricken with the appalling, disfiguring, life-destroying disease of leprosy, and so was condemned to a slow lingering death, isolated from those he loved, shunned by all. But all is not lost, for he discovers the whereabouts of someone who might cure him, through the words of a slave girl captured by the Syrians. Naaman shows his desperation for a cure, in that he is prepared to act on the words of the most insignificant member of his household, if they hold out even the slightest chance of a cure. So Naaman goes to Elisha, and is snubbed, quite severely. Naaman, a man of great stature, has already lowered himself considerably to go to the house of the prophet, instead of summoning Elisha to his own home. But even then Elisha does not go out to meet him, but sends a messenger with instructions for Naaman's cure. It is this that proves to be the final straw, for all Naaman has to do is bathe in the River Jordan seven times and he will be healed. Naaman cannot believe this – surely a man of his social and economic standing, with a disease of such magnitude, should need a cure that is challenging and complicated, or at least expensive! This arrogance nearly proves his undoing, but he is rescued once again by servants and submits to the indignity of bathing in a muddy river and is healed.

Naaman nearly missed out on a cure, on the chance of wholeness, because initially he failed to realize that it is through the small things, the ordinary acts of daily life, undertaken in obedience to God, that God can accomplish great things within us and through us. They may not always be the great things that we would have chosen, or that we expected, but if we are faithful and prayerful and trust right up to the seventh immersion, then we will indeed be healed.

EXERCISE

One of the greatest gifts of the natural world is that of water, and we are fortunate in this part of the world that we have unlimited access to clean, running water. At the end of the day, set aside some time to wash your hands slowly and mindfully. Prepare the space beforehand, laying out a clean towel and some nice soap. Allow the water to run into the basin, noticing how it sparkles and dances as it flows. When the basin is full, immerse your hands, feeling the sensation of water on your skin. Wash your hands slowly and carefully, noticing the bubbles of the soap, the feeling of your hands rubbing against each other. Become aware of each finger in turn as you wash it clean. Remember Naaman, washing away the disease of leprosy and how he must have felt as his skin grew whole again. You might think of some of the words and actions of your day that you would like to be cleansed of, or the words and actions of others that should not cling to you but be washed away. Empty the water and rinse the basin, letting the dirty water disappear, then dry your hands slowly and carefully.

Knit together in love
PSALM 139.1–18

O Lord, you have searched me and known me.
You know when I sit down and when I rise up;
you discern my thoughts from far away.
You search out my path and my lying down,
and are acquainted with all my ways.
Even before a word is on my tongue,
O Lord, you know it completely.
You hem me in, behind and before,
and lay your hand upon me.
Such knowledge is too wonderful for me;
it is so high that I cannot attain it.

Where can I go from your spirit?
Or where can I flee from your presence?
If I ascend to heaven, you are there;
if I make my bed in Sheol, you are there.
If I take the wings of the morning
and settle at the farthest limits of the sea,
even there your hand shall lead me,
and your right hand shall hold me fast.
If I say, 'Surely the darkness shall cover me,
and the light around me become night',
even the darkness is not dark to you;
the night is as bright as the day,
for darkness is as light to you.

For it was you who formed my inward parts;
you knit me together in my mother's womb.
I praise you, for I am fearfully and wonderfully made.
Wonderful are your works;
that I know very well.
My frame was not hidden from you,
when I was being made in secret,

intricately woven in the depths of the earth.
Your eyes beheld my unformed substance.
In your book were written
all the days that were formed for me,
when none of them as yet existed.
How weighty to me are your thoughts, O God!
How vast is the sum of them!
I try to count them – they are more than the sand;
I come to the end – I am still with you.

The life of King David could certainly not be described as an easy one, even though his triumphal ascent from shepherd boy to king might seem to be the traditional 'rags to riches' tale. Some of the disasters that befell him were of his own making – his deceit with regard to Bathsheba, and his cruel plots against her husband Uriah, arranging matters so that his death was almost inevitable, being but one example. Other disasters, though, were not of his doing, but the result of the actions of his enemies and those whom he had thought his friends. It might be easy to suppose that during his many days and nights in hiding, camped out in damp caves or roaming the desert landscape, that David would be tempted to spend much time wondering how it had gone so wrong and what he had done to deserve the many hardships that befell him. However, his songs, the Psalms, tell a different story. For in the midst of his misfortunes, David knows that he is not alone. He is aware of a loving presence that will sustain him and carry him through any number of disasters, and it is to this presence that he turns in both triumph and sadness. Psalm 139 is full of the security that is formed by knowing that one is completely and truly loved. Even before birth, God wraps us in his love; he knows us intimately, both the good and the bad – there is nothing about us that can shock him or turn him away from us. We are held and sustained through our darkest times – we only have to turn to God and there will be light.

When we are unhappy or stressed, the temptation is to worry about the situation, to try to work out why we feel this way, and to put measures in place to change it. Sometimes, action is needed, and we do need to take hold of our lives and arrange matters in the way that they should be. On other occasions, however, there is nothing that can be done about our situation. During these times, we can turn to God and remember the care he took over our creation, and the love he has for us. Stepping outside the preoccupations of our minds, tangled as they might be with fear and anxiety, we can relax in God's loving arms and find there the strength to continue.

EXERCISE

Find a quiet and comfortable place, such as a chair or a bed. Make sure you will be warm and feel certain of not being disturbed. Make sure you feel supported and balanced in your body, relaxed but alert. Close your eyes if this helps. Take some time to 'take notice' of what is happening in your mind right now. You don't need to comment on it or judge or decide on any action; simply be aware of the thoughts and worries that are churning about. Do not allow yourself to become engaged with them; just observe them.

Now move your attention to your breath, feeling it enter and leave your body, filling your body with life. Focus on the breath as it moves in and out. If your mind wanders, do not become anxious or concerned, simply notice it and return to the breath, in and out.

Gently turn your attention to your body, becoming aware of each part in turn. Remember that God made you, that you were 'knit together' by him before you were born. Marvel at the things you can do – move, touch, see, hear. Picture yourself held in God's loving arms as he cradles you, just as a child is cradled by a mother. Know that you are loved.

Fingertip wonder
MARK 1.40–42

Now a leper came to him, imploring him, kneeling down to him and saying to him, 'If you are willing, you can make me clean.' Then Jesus, moved with compassion, stretched out his hand and touched him, and said to him, 'I am willing; be cleansed.' As soon as he had spoken, immediately the leprosy left him, and he was cleansed.

For centuries, the word 'leprosy' has held a terrible fear. This chronic bacterial infection, also known as 'Hansen's disease', may take many years to show symptoms, but when they do appear they show themselves as light and dark patches on the skin, which eventually can cause permanent damage to the skin, eyes and limbs. Secondary infections can cause fingers and hands to become deformed, and the accompanying numbness means that many injuries occur.

Nowadays, leprosy is curable, but in biblical times the appearance of the first scaly patches of skin was a death sentence. Although the physical difficulties were enormous, a greater burden was the social and psychological wounds inflicted by a society that did not understand the disease and could only fear it, and those who suffered from it. People with leprosy were isolated from the rest of the community and forced to live in separate settlements. Anyone touching them, or their clothing or personal belongings, was declared unclean, and they had to announce their presence so that others could hear they were approaching and avoid them. The man who knelt at the feet of Jesus was desperate. Separated from his home, the people he loved, dependent on the charity of others, he had to struggle with his illness alone and unsupported, with only a lonely death to look forward to. Jesus reaches out to this man, breaking through the barriers of isolation and misery, and touches him – it is perhaps the first time in many years that the man has experienced the touch of another human being. In order to

71

bring healing, Jesus once again makes himself vulnerable to infection, to contamination; he again makes himself 'unclean' in the eyes of society, preferring instead to stand alongside the outcast in compassion and love. Jesus recognized that the man in front of him was not merely a 'leper' as common parlance has it, but was a suffering human being, the same as every other person except that he carried the burden of leprosy. The power of Jesus' touch not only healed the physical distress of the man who knelt before him, but brought him back into the circle of his community, redeeming him into society, enabling him to take his place among his fellow human beings once more.

Today, although leprosy is no longer to be feared to such a degree, there are other conditions that can place us outside ordinary human society. We can become ill in mind, body or spirit, we can suffer emotional loss or distress, we can fall sick with the stress of our lives or relationships. In these situations it is easy to feel outcast and alone. At these times, we do well to remember that Jesus has chosen to break into the circle of our isolation and reach out to us in our need, and that his healing touch is available to us. We can also choose to try to act in ways that do not allow the fear of future distress or the burden of past misfortune to isolate us, but instead to focus on the moment, rejoicing in the gifts it brings.

EXERCISE

It is common knowledge that our fingertips are extremely sensitive, and recent research has shown that we can feel objects that are no bigger than 0.2mm – that is, twice the size of a human eyelash. A fingertip that is gently dragged across a surface can feel objects even smaller than that. Today, make time to truly feel some of the objects you touch. You might want to gather four or five different natural objects – such as stones, leaves, pieces of wood – and spend time slowly moving your fingers over them, noticing their curves and bumps, feeling the different textures and surfaces. Closing your eyes will help you concentrate; try to see with your fingertips, and delight in the treasures you discover.

The loving touch
LUKE 7.11–16

Soon afterwards he went to a town called Nain, and his disciples and a large crowd went with him. As he approached the gate of the town, a man who had died was being carried out. He was his mother's only son, and she was a widow; and with her was a large crowd from the town. When the Lord saw her, he had compassion for her and said to her, 'Do not weep.' Then he came forward and touched the bier, and the bearers stood still. And he said, 'Young man, I say to you, rise!' The dead man sat up and began to speak, and Jesus gave him to his mother. Fear seized all of them; and they glorified God, saying, 'A great prophet has risen among us!' and 'God has looked favourably on his people!'

For the Jewish people, a burial had to take place on the same day as the death. The body would be taken in procession on an open bier through the streets of the village or town to a place outside the settlement walls, there to be buried. Often the only way of letting a community know that a death had occurred, particularly a sudden and unexpected death, was through the procession that wound its way through the streets followed by weeping relatives, whose noise also announced the news. By the time the procession reached the gates of the town of Nain, in this case, it would have been very sizeable as all those who knew the young man and his mother would have joined in the mourning. Slowly, inexorably, the body would be led away to be buried. A mother's life would be in shreds, particularly since she was a widow and relied on her son for support – without him, she risked destitution. Then, in one moment, all expectations are changed. In front of the bier steps is Jesus, a lone figure before the crowd. While the funeral cortege looks towards the burial place and death, Jesus faces the other way and seizes life, not just for himself, but for all those who believe in him. He breaks into the traditions and customs surrounding death and touches the bier itself, and in that moment all is still. Into the stillness the word of life is spoken and all is changed. Mourning is turned to joy and restoration is complete. The reaction of the crowd is 'fear', but the sort of fear that is filled with awe and wonder. They 'glorified' God for his saving action, and rejoice with the widow and her son.

There are occasions when it seems as if we will be overcome by the inexorable nature of our lives – habits, customs and circumstances surround us and restrict us. We succumb to the noise and confusion of the secular world and allow it to overcome us. It is right, at times, to pause and seek the stillness, and then to turn and face a different way, the way of Christ, the way of life. We need to be aware of times when our pessimistic expectations are unexpectedly overturned, with joyful consequences. More importantly, we need to seek such moments, looking out for them in our daily lives, and celebrating their happening, glorifying God.

EXERCISE

Jesus breaks all traditions when he interrupts the funeral procession to touch the bier and so raise the widow's son to life. For many people, living isolated and lonely lives, touch is a rare and precious gift, and one that is lacking. Be mindful today of the people with whom you have physical contact – accidentally while travelling perhaps, or during a shopping expedition, trying on clothes, or handing over money. Pause and pray for the person, offering them to God, and asking that they may be happy. Be mindful also of the way you use touch deliberately – handshakes, hugs, caresses. Offer these to God in love, seeking always to follow his path of life, chosen in a moment of stillness.

Noticing the unnoticed ones
MARK 5.22–43

Then one of the leaders of the synagogue named Jairus came and, when he saw him, fell at his feet and begged him repeatedly, 'My little daughter is at the point of death. Come and lay your hands on her, so that she may be made well, and live.' So he went with him.

And a large crowd followed him and pressed in on him. Now there was a woman who had been suffering from haemorrhages for twelve years. She had endured much under many physicians, and had spent all that she had; and she was no better, but rather grew worse. She had heard about Jesus, and came up behind him in the crowd and touched his cloak, for she said, 'If I but touch his clothes, I will be made well.' Immediately her haemorrhage stopped; and she felt in her body that she was healed of her disease. Immediately aware that power had gone forth from him, Jesus turned about in the crowd and said, 'Who touched my clothes?'

And his disciples said to him, 'You see the crowd pressing in on you; how can you say, "Who touched me?"' He looked all round to see who had done it. But the woman, knowing what had happened to her, came in fear and trembling, fell down before him, and told him the whole truth. He said to her, 'Daughter, your faith has made you well; go in peace, and be healed of your disease.'

While he was still speaking, some people came from the leader's house to say, 'Your daughter is dead. Why trouble the teacher any further?'

But overhearing what they said, Jesus said to the leader of the synagogue, 'Do not fear, only believe.'

He allowed no one to follow him except Peter, James, and John, the brother of James. When they came to the house of the leader of the synagogue, he saw a commotion, people weeping and wailing loudly. When he had entered, he said to them, 'Why do you make a commotion and weep? The child is not dead but sleeping.' And they laughed at him.

Then he put them all outside, and took the child's father and mother and those who were with him, and went in where the child was. He took her by the hand and said to her, 'Talitha cum', which means, 'Little girl, get up!' And immediately the girl got up and began to walk about (she was twelve years of age). At this they were overcome with amazement. He strictly ordered them that no one should know this, and told them to give her something to eat.

Jesus is on his way to help the sick daughter of an elder in the synagogue. Jairus would have had wealth and privilege, his life would have been comfortable and his status secure. But he was still powerless in the face of the illness of his daughter, and with that unexpected and unpleasant powerlessness arises a willingness to look for a different path, to seek an alternative way to healing than that provided by his usual way of thinking and believing. He asks Jesus, an itinerant preacher, about whom much is rumoured, for help, and Jesus agrees to go with him. A large crowd follows, interested to see the interaction between this pillar of the establishment and the maverick preaching God's kingdom to the poor and the outcast. But even though Jesus is surrounded by people jostling and pushing at him, he can feel the desperate grasp of one woman, reaching out for healing, and he stops. He did not need to stop – no one would have known if he had not. The house he was going to would have welcomed him and rewarded him – certainly Jairus' daughter was in a bad way and desperately needed his help. But still Jesus stopped to heal a woman, an outcast, condemned by her illness to live the life of the perpetually 'unclean', on the borders of community, isolated and destitute. Anyone who touches her becomes 'unclean' themselves until the evening of that day, so no one reaches out to her – even her name has been lost. She has no wealthy father to speak for her, so she must take her future into her own hands, and touch a man in public. And this man responds, and heals. In fact he does more than heal, he restores, for not only may the woman now take part in ordinary everyday life, but she has been praised for her faith. 'Do not fear, only believe' Jesus tells those who would stop his journey, counting it already fruitless. Healing is available for rich and poor, privileged and outcast – for all who ask.

We are in danger every day of our lives of being swept along by those actions and beliefs that are considered important by the secular world. This applies to our fundamental beliefs, drawing us in to live in a worldly way, overcome by the pressure of those around us. So we treat the wealthy with more consideration and concern than the poor, or succumb to the pressure of the influential to behave as they do, ignoring the needs and the problems of those who have no power. We must allow ourselves to be taken in like this, but must follow Jesus' example, and even in the midst of the crowd we must take time to pause and listen to the voices that go unheard, those of the lost and the lonely, the underprivileged and the outcast.

EXERCISE

Take time today to pause and notice those around you, who share your lives without you even being aware of it. Stop and talk to the person who serves you coffee, who cleans the office building, who picks up litter in the street, who tries to sell you a newspaper. Treat them with respect, listen to them, share their lives for just a moment. If you have time, pause at some stage during the day and recall your encounter.

Find a place to be still and quiet. Make yourself comfortable, either sitting or lying, with your eyes open or closed, as you prefer. Still your mind and body, using the three-minute breathing exercise. Then bring to your attention someone you encountered today. Imagine them cradled in the hand of God, being held and supported by him, cared for by him out of his great love. Pray for them, that they may be happy and at peace. You could pray on an in breath, addressing them directly: 'May you find peace' or 'May you be happy' or simply 'God is with you'. Focus on the fact of their being a child of God, God's creation. When you are ready, leave them with God and bring your mind again to the sensation of the breath entering and leaving your body.

TASTE

Resisting the pattern of the world
GENESIS 3.1–7

*Now the serpent was more crafty than any other wild animal
that the Lord God had made. He said to the woman, 'Did
God say, "You shall not eat from any tree in the garden"?'
The woman said to the serpent, 'We may eat of the fruit of
the trees in the garden; but God said, "You shall not eat of
the fruit of the tree that is in the middle of the garden, nor
shall you touch it, or you shall die."'*

*But the serpent said to the woman, 'You will not die; for
God knows that when you eat of it your eyes will be opened,
and you will be like God, knowing good and evil.'*

*So when the woman saw that the tree was good for food,
and that it was a delight to the eyes, and that the tree was
to be desired to make one wise, she took of its fruit and
ate; and she also gave some to her husband, who was with
her, and he ate. Then the eyes of both were opened, and
they knew that they were naked; and they sewed fig leaves
together and made loincloths for themselves.*

Although the fruit that was eaten is not specified here,
traditionally this story has become the most famous apple-
tasting scene there is. At the heart of the story is our relationship
with God, formed out of love and built on trust. God loves
all people and wants the best for them; a close and living
relationship with him through Christ in the power of the Holy
Spirit. However, this relationship cannot be forced on us; we
can be held to it through nothing but our own free will. We have

been given the gift of freedom and it is up to each individual to choose how to use that freedom. God longs for us to come to him, but we must do so willingly, without being compelled. We must be obedient to God's way even when he appears to be absent – remember that God only walks in the Garden in the evening, and the rest of the time Adam and Eve have to trust his word, just as we do. It is in those times of apparent absence that the voices of the external, secular world shout loudly, calling to us of the attractions of wealth, power, status, material possessions as alternative gods, tangible objectives that have the approval of the world and are easier to obtain and have more obvious rewards than the dubious uncertainty of a relationship with an invisible God. The fruit represents those worldly temptations that call us away from the right path; the serpent's voice the voices we hear, both from those around us and within our own heads. They tell us that we can manage by ourselves, we do not need God or anyone else. They encourage us to aim for a cynical self-sufficiency, hardened against the claims of our spiritual needs and those of others. We are enticed into a proclamation of independence from God and from our fellow human beings, ignoring the whisperings of our heart's seeking and aiming for the easier, more straightforward goals of this world, rather than engaging in the nebulous search for those of the next. When we are tempted, in the noise and the heat of the day's activities, to cease our striving and fall into the pattern of the world, we must find time to remember the cool of the evening, to recreate the peace and calm in our hearts and seek God, who is 'walking in the garden at the time of the evening breeze' (Genesis 3.8A), coming towards us to meet us, just as we go forward to meet him.

EXERCISE

When we are in danger of being seduced by the attractions that the world can offer, such delights can seem hard to resist. The charm of power, the ease of wealth, the luxury of possessions, are very seductive. So too is the opposite impulse, to head away from God not towards an apparently more attractive goal, but away from the difficulties and setbacks that entering into a relationship with him and with fellow Christians entail. At such times, a brief pause, a moment to step back from the external, can be all that is needed to rebuild and renew our confidence in the one who is always present, whether we are aware of him or not.

Find a comfortable place to sit or lie – if this is not possible, find somewhere you can stand undisturbed for a short time. Make sure you feel supported and balanced in your body, relaxed but alert. Close your eyes if this helps. Take some time to 'take notice' of what is happening in your mind right now. You don't need to comment on it or judge or decide on any action, simply be aware of the thoughts and worries that are churning around. Do not allow yourself to become engaged with them; just observe them.

Now move your attention to your breath, feeling it enter and leave your body, filling your body with life. Focus on the breath as it moves in and out. If your mind wanders, do not become anxious or concerned, simply take notice and return to the breath, in and out.

On your out breath you might like to breathe the word YHWH, allowing it to become part of your exhalation. Let the breath become your prayer, your answering call to the reassurance and love of the breath of God as it fills your whole body; 'This is my name for ever, and this my title for all generations' (Exodus 3.15).

Come to the waters
ISAIAH 55.1–3, 10, 11

> *Ho, everyone who thirsts,*
> *come to the waters;*
> *and you that have no money,*
> *come, buy and eat!*
> *Come, buy wine and milk*
> *without money and without price …*
> *For as the rain and the snow come down from heaven,*
> *and do not return there until they have watered the earth,*
> *making it bring forth and sprout,*
> *giving seed to the sower and bread to the eater,*
> *so shall my word be that goes out from my mouth;*
> *it shall not return to me empty,*
> *but it shall accomplish that which I purpose,*
> *and succeed in the thing for which I sent it.*

Oceans cover nearly three-quarters of the world's surface, and they are home to most of the creatures that live on this planet. Water plays a significant part in regulating our climate and in absorbing carbon dioxide, a vital role in the natural systems of the world. Water is found in all living and most non-living matter and is essential for our survival. The earliest settlements of human beings grew up alongside natural watercourses such as rivers and streams, or gathered around lakes and wells. The types of crops grown and industries worked depend on the amount of water available and influence the success not just of a community but of a country. Much of the wealth and power of the United Kingdom during the nineteenth and twentieth centuries stemmed from water-driven industries providing potential for feeding and clothing large numbers of people. Today, in this country, fresh, clean water is instantly and plentifully available, and it is easy to take it for granted, but this would be to ignore a precious and vital gift. The poem in Isaiah reminds us of what it feels like to be thirsty, how uncomfortable and ultimately life-threatening this can be. It reminds us too of the vital part that water plays in providing food for us to eat. Water becomes a metaphor for our spiritual thirst, our longing to find the source of life and drink deeply from it, replenishing and resourcing our inner selves for our life's journey. With the generosity that is characteristic of God, we are invited to partake freely of all the good things that he has to offer, feeding both our bodies and our souls.

EXERCISE

This can be practised at any time of day, whenever you stop for a hot drink.

First, choose the cup or mug you will use. Choose carefully and thoughtfully – make sure it fits its purpose: the right size, the right material. Place it carefully next to the kettle.

Fill the kettle with water, noticing how clear and cold the water is, how fast it rushes in. Pray for those who do not have fresh water easily available, for whom the search for water takes up most of the day's effort and time.

While the kettle is boiling, stand still and breathe deeply and gently. Remember the phrase of Hildegard of Bingen 'I am a feather on the breath of God', and say this while you breathe in and out.

Make your drink and take time to watch the steam rise from the cup. Add milk if you wish, watching the way the two liquids merge and combine.

Drink slowly and thoughtfully. Focus all your attention on what you are doing. Feel the warmth of the cup in your hands, smell the fragrance of your drink, its combination of scents. Taste the flavour, allowing it to rest on your tongue.

Remember that 'we are God's children now' (1 John 3.2).

Take time to enjoy the presence of God, to rest in his

love, and to shelter in his arms; 'what we will be has not yet been revealed' (1 John 3.2), but we can trust in his love and find peace in the fact that the past is behind us and the future is safe in God's hands.

Taste and see
PSALM 34.1–8

> *I will bless the Lord at all times;*
> *his praise shall continually be in my mouth.*
> *My soul makes its boast in the Lord;*
> *let the humble hear and be glad.*
> *O magnify the Lord with me,*
> *and let us exalt his name together.*
> *I sought the Lord, and he answered me,*
> *and delivered me from all my fears.*
> *Look to him, and be radiant;*
> *so your faces shall never be ashamed.*
> *This poor soul cried, and was heard by the Lord,*
> *and was saved from every trouble.*
> *The angel of the Lord encamps*
> *around those who fear him, and delivers them.*
> *O taste and see that the Lord is good;*
> *happy are those who take refuge in him.*

What an interesting concept – to 'taste and see that the Lord is good'! At first reading this appears to be an impossibility, as it seems as if we cannot experience God in this way. But every time we put food into our mouths, we are experiencing the goodness of God in his loving provision for us. Our celebration of the gift of food, of its variety of tastes and textures, should not be confined to harvest time, but become a daily habit, as we thank God for his imaginative act of creation in the wonderful range of food available to us, even the simplest forms being charged with flavour.

But the Hebrew word that is translated as 'taste' in this psalm means not just simply the action of eating, but also the process of trying the flavour of something, to test it by experiencing it. We are being invited to try and experience God's goodness to us, born from his great love for us, just as we might try out a new food. This might be done hesitantly and tentatively at first, but happens with growing confidence as we become familiar with the flavour and texture of the new food. We become gradually more confident that it tastes good, and eager to repeat the experience. So too, when we acknowledge the goodness of God, when we first begin to put our trust in him, believing that he will care for us with tenderness and love, we might begin cautiously. We might hesitate to put all our trust in him initially, but then, when time after time God's love for us illuminates our daily lives, we grow more confident – so we can face our fears and anxieties with a mind uncluttered by past memories, unshadowed with foreboding, or the fretful imaginings of possible unpleasant outcomes. Instead we trust in the Lord, giving thanks for those previous occasions when we have been delivered from our fears, and taking refuge in his love.

EXERCISE

Choose an occasion when you know you will have plenty of time to eat your meal. You might wish to invite someone to share your meal, emphasizing that it will be a special occasion, or you might wish to undertake this exercise on your own. Plan the meal in detail, choosing food that is both healthy and that you enjoy eating. Prepare it carefully and, if you are able, set a table so that you can eat it with some degree of formality. Once you have cooked your meal and it is completely ready, place it on the table, and serve yourself a plateful. Then for a period of one or two minutes, simply pause and look at the food you are about to eat. Notice the colours of the different foodstuffs, and how they complement one another. Look at the various textures that are on your plate and the different sized portions of the food you are about to eat. Reflect on the miracle of planting, growth, harvest and preparation that have led to this meal, and give thanks to God for its creation, praying also for all those who worked with God in its cultivation and preparation.

Called to act
MATTHEW 14.13–21

Now when Jesus heard this, he withdrew from there in a boat to a deserted place by himself. But when the crowds heard it, they followed him on foot from the towns. When he went ashore, he saw a great crowd; and he had compassion for them and cured their sick.

When it was evening, the disciples came to him and said, 'This is a deserted place, and the hour is now late; send the crowds away so that they may go into the villages and buy food for themselves.'

Jesus said to them, 'They need not go away; you give them something to eat.'

They replied, 'We have nothing here but five loaves and two fish.'

And he said, 'Bring them here to me.' Then he ordered the crowds to sit down on the grass. Taking the five loaves and the two fish, he looked up to heaven, and blessed and broke the loaves, and gave them to the disciples, and the disciples gave them to the crowds. And all ate and were filled; and they took up what was left over of the broken pieces, twelve baskets full. And those who ate were about five thousand men, besides women and children.

The most challenging aspect of this story is not merely within its content, but in the fact that we are so familiar with it that we are in danger of ignoring the truths held within it. Mindful Bible reading encourages us to look again at familiar passages and read them carefully and attentively, seeing them with new eyes and hearing the word of God as if it were freshly written, specifically for us and for our time. This story shares with us many truths about gospel living – one of the most vibrant and life-giving being in the very way we view those things within our lives that we consider the most ordinary.

In a primary school classroom, a question was asked by the teacher: 'If you were stuck on a desert island for a fortnight, who would you like to be your companion?' There were many different answers – Bear Grylls, the survival expert, a best friend, a dad. One boy, however, answered, 'I would choose the President of the United States, because then I would not be stuck there for two weeks, as the whole world would be searching for us.'

The disciples are faced with a problem – five thousand people and no food. To them the solution is simple – to tell them there is no food, and to go away. But Jesus charges them to think again, to think differently, to think with the eyes of faith. There isn't always a different answer, but sometimes, looking with new eyes, the eyes of faith, of love, of compassion, can help us find an unexpected solution – remember that Jesus began to teach the crowd because he had compassion for them.

However, for a miracle to happen, we need to play our part. Every miracle is the result of a relationship between God and the recipient of the miracle. When the disciples approach Jesus with the problem of the crowd, he turns it back to them: 'you give them something to eat'. Their first impulse is to reject this – 'We have nothing here but five loaves and two fish.' How many times have we heard this response or said it ourselves when faced with a social or political crisis? How can we help with what little we have? We don't even know how we will make do ourselves! More damagingly we say this about ourselves, and our emotional and spiritual resources, when confronted with the problems of caring for others or for ourselves: 'We don't have enough time, or energy, we aren't wise enough, we don't have the training, we won't make any difference.' But God knows all that, and still calls us to play our part. For he needs us to play our part so that he can play his, so that he can take the little we have and multiply it so that there is enough.

EXERCISE

Next time you are preparing a meal, try to consider it in a new light. If possible, it should be a meal that is cooked by yourself, rather than one that only requires microwaving. Even a simple meal such as a boiled egg and toast can be prepared with attention and love. Slow down your actions, even those with which you are so familiar they are second nature. Notice the texture and colour of the food you are preparing, and how it gradually changes as it progresses through the cooking process. When the meal is ready, arrange it attractively on a plate, and take a few minutes to consider the miracles of germination and cultivation that have gone into its creation. You might wish to say a simple prayer of thanks before beginning to eat.

There is an apocryphal story about Mother Teresa of Calcutta, who wanted to build an orphanage. She told her superiors, 'I have three pennies and a dream from God to build an orphanage.'

'Mother Teresa,' her superiors chided gently, 'you cannot build an orphanage with three pennies … with three pennies you can't do much at all.'

'I know,' she said, smiling, 'but with God and three pennies I can do anything.'

Extract the full meaning
MATTHEW 26.36–46

Then Jesus went with them to a place called Gethsemane; and he said to his disciples, 'Sit here while I go over there and pray.' He took with him Peter and the two sons of Zebedee, and began to be grieved and agitated. Then he said to them, 'I am deeply grieved, even to death; remain here, and stay awake with me.'

And going a little farther, he threw himself on the ground and prayed, 'My Father, if it is possible, let this cup pass from me; yet not what I want but what you want.'

Then he came to the disciples and found them sleeping; and he said to Peter, 'So, could you not stay awake with me one hour? Stay awake and pray that you may not come into the time of trial; the spirit indeed is willing, but the flesh is weak.'

Again he went away for the second time and prayed, 'My Father, if this cannot pass unless I drink it, your will be done.'

Again he came and found them sleeping, for their eyes were heavy. So leaving them again, he went away and prayed for the third time, saying the same words.

Then he came to the disciples and said to them, 'Are you still sleeping and taking your rest? See, the hour is at hand, and the Son of Man is betrayed into the hands of sinners. Get up, let us be going. See, my betrayer is at hand.'

This passage very often does not get the attention it deserves, since it comes in the middle of the story of the Passion, and events crowding in one after another mean that the quiet, reflective times often get missed out for the sake of the noisier drama. Yet in the Garden of Gethsemane, Eden is redeemed and heaven is foretold, as Jesus kneels and reaffirms his covenant with his Father for the sake of our salvation.

It was in a garden that our ancestor Adam first chose the

path against God and the relationship between them was broken. Adam's disobedience opened the path for sin and death, a path that led to the Garden in which Jesus now kneels to pray, in an agony of grief. He pleads with his companions to remain awake and watch with him, but they do not do so; while he faces and resists the greatest of temptations, Peter, James and John succumb to their considerably lesser one and fall asleep, failing in the simple task that was asked of them. They miss that vital, history-making moment, when Christ accepts his part in the redemption of all human beings and takes upon himself their sin and consequent suffering. For them, the link is broken, but there is one stronger who holds together the sinful past of Eden and looks to the heavenly garden of Revelation (Revelation 22.1), which includes the 'river of the water of life, bright as crystal, flowing from the throne of God and of the Lamb' and 'the tree of life ... producing its fruit', and whose 'leaves of the tree are for the healing of the nations' (Revelation 22.2). It is through Christ's willingness to drink from the cup that contains the bitter waters of death that the failure of his disciples is redeemed, along with the failure of all the children of God to watch and wait for the coming of the kingdom.

So much of what we do and say is undertaken automatically – everyday tasks and conversations, journeys and experiences, are repeated daily, hourly even, until a thick layer of familiarity is built up upon the event, obscuring its true nature beneath a history of previous actions and events. So too must Peter, James and John have treated the habit of Jesus in going away to pray. The Gospels are filled with references to Jesus distancing himself from those around him and retreating to spend time alone with God. This time is different, however; he asks for their company. He asks that they might be alongside him as he prepares to accept the cup that has been passed to him, from which it is his duty to drink. But the disciples are still expecting the event to be the same as every other time, and perhaps they look forward to a time of rest and a chance to restore their energy. Whatever their reason, they do not do as they are asked, and they miss out.

EXERCISE

Take one task, journey or activity that you do every day, and do it mindfully today. Put all your attention into what you are doing – whether it is as simple a thing as cleaning your teeth, or driving to work, or clearing the table. Notice the actions that make up the activity, the sensations of objects in your hands as you use them, your movements as you carry out the activity. If your mind drifts away from what you are doing, it doesn't matter; just notice that it has and focus once more on your task. Reach deep into the task to extract its full meaning, and expand into the moment.

THE PASSION

The following reflections explore the events leading up to Jesus' death and resurrection through the five senses and through silence. They are particularly appropriate for Holy Week and Easter, but can be used at any time of the year.

PALM SUNDAY

Cherish each sound
MATTHEW 21.1-9

When they had come near Jerusalem and had reached Bethphage, at the Mount of Olives, Jesus sent two disciples, saying to them, 'Go into the village ahead of you, and immediately you will find a donkey tied, and a colt with her; untie them and bring them to me. If anyone says anything to you, just say this, "The Lord needs them." And he will send them immediately.' This took place to fulfil what had been spoken through the prophet, saying,

> *'Tell the daughter of Zion,*
> *Look, your king is coming to you,*
> *humble, and mounted on a donkey,*
> *and on a colt, the foal of a donkey.'*

The disciples went and did as Jesus had directed them; they brought the donkey and the colt, and put their cloaks on them, and he sat on them. A very large crowd spread their cloaks on the road, and others cut branches from the trees and spread them on the road. The crowds that went ahead of him and that followed were shouting,

> *'Hosana to the Son of David!*
> *Blessed is the one who comes in the name of the Lord!*
> *Hosanna in the highest heaven!'*

'Hosanna to the Son of David' – shouting, calling out to Jesus, waving palm branches, this is what we remember about Palm Sunday. The noise must have been tremendous – the crowds were gathered in Jerusalem ready to celebrate the Passover, everyone was in a holiday mood, and the atmosphere was ripe for a party. What better way to celebrate than to join a parade? And indeed, there is nothing wrong in this at all, celebrations and gatherings add colour to our lives; they are something to look forward to and plan for amid the regular routine. Because routine there certainly is, and this is often overlooked when studying this episode from Christ's life. For before he could enter Jerusalem, a donkey had to be found, and it was the disciples' task to find it.

Much detail is given to recounting this job – Jesus tells the disciples where to go, what to do and to say, and they dutifully bring back the animals. It is interesting to wonder what the disciples felt about doing this; perhaps they had imagined a grander role for themselves on the day of Jesus' entry into Jerusalem. Throughout their time with Jesus, disputes had arisen as to who was the greatest, who would sit beside Jesus in heaven, who would share the glory. How very down to earth were the jobs they were given – getting a boat ready, feeding a crowd, preparing a room for a meal. The disciples must have wondered why they had left their fishing nets!

Very often in our lives we find ourselves relegated to the routine and inglorious tasks that are necessary but not exciting, important but not interesting, and this can be disappointing indeed. It can often be a sad disillusion to discover that serving the people of God comes down to fewer glorious conversion moments and more washing up of cups, tidying toys, visiting people in nursing homes, removing half-eaten biscuits from the pews – and, as two of Jesus' disciples found out, finding a suitable donkey at the last minute. But by entering into the moment of these tasks, undertaking them mindfully, aware of every action, taking care over every detail, we can fully inhabit the present. We can relish the task, focusing not only on its results, but on the preparation, offering the moment to God. 'Preparing the way for the Lord' is often made up of performing humble and ordinary tasks – those exhausting, seemingly mundane, donkey-fetching details of service that become, through God's grace, part of the redemptive work of bringing nearer the kingdom of heaven. For even Jesus is not beyond washing feet, sitting by a well, or cooking fish at a lakeside.

EXERCISE

Find a comfortable place to sit or lie – or if not possible, somewhere you can stand undisturbed for a short time. Make sure you feel supported and balanced in your body, relaxed but alert. Close your eyes if this helps. Focus your mind on your breath, feeling it enter and leave your body, filling your body with life. Focus on the breath as it moves in and out. If your mind wanders, do not become anxious or concerned; simply take note of it and return to the breath, in and out.

Now move your attention to the sounds you hear around you. Don't try to analyse them or describe them; it isn't necessary to define what the sound is or what has made it. Simply hear the sound for what it is. Notice its length, its loudness, whether it is harmonious to the ear or discordant. If your mind wanders, and you find yourself trying to define the sound, do not be concerned, simply allow the sound to pass by. Cherish each sound, however slight; be aware of its beauty and its life.

If you wish, you can then turn your attention to the thoughts that are going through your mind, and treat them in the same way. Notice them when they appear in your mind, but do not try to define them or give them a story or a background. Simply allow them to come and go, just as the sounds around you rise and fade in intensity. If you become anxious or distressed, notice this, but let them be as they are.

Return your attention to your breath when you have finished, bringing your mind back to the present moment.

HOLY WEEK MONDAY

Observe in truth
JOHN 12.1-8

> *Then, six days before the Passover, Jesus came to Bethany,*
> *where Lazarus was who had been dead, whom he had*
> *raised from the dead. There they made him a supper; and*
> *Martha served, but Lazarus was one of those who sat at the*
> *table with him. Then Mary took a pound of very costly oil*
> *of spikenard, anointed the feet of Jesus, and wiped his feet*
> *with her hair. And the house was filled with the fragrance*
> *of the oil.*
>
> *But one of his disciples, Judas Iscariot, Simon's son, who*
> *would betray him, said, 'Why was this fragrant oil not sold*
> *for three hundred denarii and given to the poor?' This he*
> *said, not that he cared for the poor, but because he was a*
> *thief, and had the money box; and he used to take what was*
> *put in it.*
>
> *But Jesus said, 'Let her alone; she has kept this for the*
> *day of my burial. For the poor you have with you always,*
> *but me you do not have always.'*

How shocked the disciples must have been at the action of
Mary! For a woman to abandon her role of serving the men at
supper was a breach of decorum, but to follow this by anointing
his feet was scandal indeed. And as for wiping his feet with her
hair, that symbol of women's sexuality, usually kept covered for
modesty's sake – truly all the conventions were being flouted!
The disciples must have been used to the unconventionality

of Jesus' actions by now; they probably thought they had seen just about everything, but once again he was showing them a different way. For Jesus had recognized the impulse behind Mary's actions, an impulse of love and gratitude, stemming from the time she has spent in Jesus' company, and his bringing of Lazarus back from the dead. He can discern the truth that lies within her deeds, he is able to set aside the appearance of wrongdoing, of the infringement of custom, and perceive the light of love that guides her actions. Judas Iscariot, whose mind, we are told, has already been corrupted and who has set out along the path that will lead to his betrayal of Jesus, cannot see this truth. He is concerned only with the externals of her action and is correspondingly shocked and angry.

There are many occasions in our lives when we must deal with people and situations that we find challenging and unpleasant. Often it is our anticipation of these events that causes the most stress – looking back through our memories of previous encounters or past experiences, we are tempted to extrapolate from them to anticipate the unfolding of events in a particular way in the future. This anxious projecting can prevent us from discerning the truth of a person's actions, from seeing them actually as they are rather than as we fear they might be. Fearful foreboding can stop us from perceiving a situation as it really is, rather than one that is hung round with the mists of conjecture and possibility. If we are able to step back from our emotions, to observe the reality of what is happening in a way that is objective and freed from our imaginings, then the picture we gain will be the more truthful.

EXERCISE

If you are in the midst of a situation that you find stressful, or have dealings with a person whom you find difficult, it can be very hard to stop the headlong flight of emotions and feelings that you are experiencing. Ideally, the opportunity should be taken to distance yourself from the event or person for a short while, and practise the three-minute breathing space. This will give you time to centre yourself, and to remember to focus on what is actually happening, the event as it is unfolding rather than as you fear it might. In reality, finding this time might be impossible. Instead, try to focus on a specific observation or fact about the person or situation that is proving distressing. Notice the colour of the person's hair, remind yourself of a fact about them that you know – their age, their hobbies, where they live. Notice the surroundings that you are in: the colour of the walls or the landscape, the temperature. This way, you can bring your mind back to the present moment and be better equipped to perceive the truth within as to what is happening. Once the truth has been observed, it can be faced and appropriate action – or inaction – taken.

HOLY WEEK TUESDAY

Two small coins
MARK 12.41–44

> *He sat down opposite the treasury, and watched the crowd putting money into the treasury. Many rich people put in large sums. A poor widow came and put in two small copper coins, which are worth a penny.*
>
> *Then he called his disciples and said to them, 'Truly I tell you, this poor widow has put in more than all those who are contributing to the treasury. For all of them have contributed out of their abundance; but she out of her poverty has put in everything she had, all she had to live on.'*

One of the popular complaints about the Church is that it is always out to get people's money. Certainly the amount of attention focused on fund raising, charitable giving and financial statements would seem to support this contention, much to the detriment of the gospel message. A similar distraction has been the various discussions over how much money an individual should give to their church community, whether tithing refers to 10 per cent or 1 per cent of an income, whether this income is gross or net, whether an individual can influence how the money is spent. Things were no different in New Testament times, and Jesus' comments are sharp and to the point – there is nothing wrong with gaining wealth honestly; but, once gained, it should not be hoarded or withheld from a lack of generosity towards others. But there is more to Christian living than simply deciding how much to donate to a church; for everything we have comes from the God who created us and belongs to him.

When we give to our community we are returning what was loaned to us. Therefore we must consider not just what we give to the church, but how the rest of our spending might honour God. The two small coins of the widow in Mark 12 are infinitely precious to God because she has made over all her wealth to the one who first bestowed it upon her; not one farthing has been kept, unlike the actions of the wealthy donors who are careful to set aside a portion of their income for their own personal pleasure. So too we must give not just a portion of our lives to God, but all of them. It is not enough to honour God simply on a Sunday morning, or simply in our tithing or our charitable works; our Mondays to Saturdays must do the same, our regular activities, our leisure, must all bear witness to God's love for us and our response to that love. Living in the moment, by rejoicing in every instant of life that has been given to us, we can honour our creator. By celebrating the small happinesses that occur in our lives, we can focus on the 'glory' moments and divert energy and attention away from those things that deplete our physical and emotional resources.

EXERCISE

Set yourself a target of recording in words or pictures a happy moment every day. Decide how long you want this project to last – a week, a month, or even 40 days. The moments can be small or great – a plate of your favourite food, the smile of one who loves you, a good film, or a party, a celebration, a success. Even in times of great struggle or sadness, beauty and joy can be found in the song of a bird, the warmth of sunshine on the face, or the comfort of a hot cup of tea. Your moments do not have to be wildly varied, but they must be recorded daily, for every moment is individual and precious. At the end of the project, spend some time looking back over your happy moments and thank God for his gifts.

HOLY WEEK WEDNESDAY

'Are you going to wash my feet?'
JOHN 13.1–11

Now before the festival of the Passover, Jesus knew that his hour had come to depart from this world and go to the Father. Having loved his own who were in the world, he loved them to the end. The devil had already put it into the heart of Judas son of Simon Iscariot to betray him. And during supper Jesus, knowing that the Father had given all things into his hands, and that he had come from God and was going to God, got up from the table, took off his outer robe, and tied a towel around himself. Then he poured water into a basin and began to wash the disciples' feet and to wipe them with the towel that was tied around him. He came to Simon Peter, who said to him, 'Lord, are you going to wash my feet?' Jesus answered, 'You do not know now what I am doing, but later you will understand.' Peter said to him, 'You will never wash my feet.' Jesus answered, 'Unless I wash you, you have no share with me.' Simon Peter said to him, 'Lord, not my feet only but also my hands and my head!' Jesus said to him, 'One who has bathed does not need to wash, except for the feet, but is entirely clean. And you are clean, though not all of you.' For he knew who was to betray him; for this reason he said, 'Not all of you are clean.'

The landscape around Jerusalem is beautiful, but harsh. Stony dry soil, with rocky outcrops and small shrubs, lines the rough track that leads into the city. The track itself is dusty and dirty, with stones that bruise the feet and piles of animal dung to be avoided. At the time of the Passover, it would have been crowded as well, and harder to avoid the heaps of dirt or uneven patches. By the time the disciples reached the room where they were to eat supper, they would have been hot and tired, eager to stretch out and rest a while, and keen to wash off the dust and dirt of the journey. Imagine their surprise when instead of the traditional servant, their master himself knelt down to wash their feet, calloused and rough from walking so many miles in coarse, ill-fitting sandals, covered in dust and worse from the journey. The usual way of things, as was so often the case with Jesus, was being turned upside down. But how cool that water must have felt on their hot, tired bodies, how gentle the touch of love that carefully wiped away all stains from the journey. All of Jesus' love and care for his disciples could be felt in the way he cradled their feet in his hands, all the hopes he had for them and their mission to spread the good news of God's love to all people, all the prayers for their future. In that one humble, caring action, Jesus embodied his message of hope and love, communicating more clearly than words, with a gesture of servanthood and compassion.

Sometimes all it takes for us to communicate our feelings is a gentle touch of kindness. We need not be too proud to serve others, for Jesus first served us in ways greater than we can ever imagine. We need not be too proud to accept the service of others, for it is through this that we become part of the community of the gospel.

EXERCISE

Find a quiet space where you can be still and comfortable. This can be sitting or lying, but it should be somewhere you can be still for a sustained period of time. Settle yourself so that you will remain alert and aware, and slow

103

your breathing, gradually becoming aware of your physical surroundings – where your body touches your chair or the surface on which you are lying, how you feel within your clothes.

Beginning with your toes, try to discern any sensation or feeling in them. Don't worry if you feel nothing, sometimes this comes with continued practice of the body scan. If you feel discomfort in your toes, notice this. Try not to become involved in analysing the sensation or worrying about it, simply be aware of it without judging, allowing it to be what it is.

Deepen your breathing, becoming aware of your breath flowing throughout your entire body, filling every blood cell with oxygen, sustaining life.

Don't worry if your mind wanders – it probably will. When it does, simply bring it back to the task in hand, the task of the present, and continue your journey round your body.

Gradually move your attention from your toes to your feet, feeling the textures of material that they are resting on, becoming aware of the skin covering them. You may want to picture Christ washing them gently, holding your feet in his hands as he dries them with a towel, showing his care for you in his gestures.

When you have finished, focus on your breathing and spend some time simply being aware of your breath as it enters and leaves your body.

MAUNDY THURSDAY

Living without appropriating
LUKE 22.14–20

When the hour came, he took his place at the table, and the apostles with him. He said to them, 'I have eagerly desired to eat this Passover with you before I suffer; for I tell you, I will not eat it until it is fulfilled in the kingdom of God.' Then he took a cup, and after giving thanks he said, 'Take this and divide it among yourselves; for I tell you that from now on I will not drink of the fruit of the vine until the kingdom of God comes.' Then he took a loaf of bread, and when he had given thanks, he broke it and gave it to them, saying, 'This is my body, which is given for you. Do this in remembrance of me.' And he did the same with the cup after supper, saying, 'This cup that is poured out for you is the new covenant in my blood.'

Francesco di Bernardone, founder of the Franciscan order of monks, was born in Assisi in Umbria in about 1181, and died there on 3 October 1226. He is better known to us as St Francis. Born into a wealthy merchant family, Francis decided to take literally the command of Christ to 'take nothing for the journey' and renounced all material goods, not even keeping a spare robe or pair of sandals. Ever since then, poverty has been a cornerstone of Franciscan spirituality. St Francis, and later his band of followers, either worked or begged for the small amount of food they needed to sustain life and gave away the rest – or all of it if it was required by someone in more severe circumstances than they were. No doubt influenced by his childhood in the house of a merchant to whom material possessions were not only a symbol of status, but in themselves the means by which more was accumulated, Francis saw all material goods as intense obstacles to a life of communion with Christ. Things, stuff, objects, that fill up our lives gradually become by the weight and mass of their existence a physical barrier to spiritual freedom. Money, possessions, status – the acquiring of all these things demands energy, time and focus, which Francis felt would be better directed towards praising God and living in his presence. The acquisition of objects involves fear – with accumulation comes fear of loss and the consequent struggle to retain a grip on what are far from being necessities for our existence. Liberated from the struggles to acquire and the fear of subsequent loss, Francis would move lightly through the world, unhindered by baggage.

For most of us today a similar dramatic shedding of all our material goods and responsibilities would not only be almost impossible, it would be inadvisable. But there is a middle path to be explored, a way that treads carefully through the landscape cluttered with unnecessary material and status objects, taking them without linking oneself to their value, appreciating them without becoming defined by them, sitting lightly to the benefits and disadvantages that they bring. Francis called such living 'vivere sine proprio' – living without appropriating. For him it meant living without possessing anything; for those who wish to tread in Francis' footsteps we need only seek to live without being possessed by anything. Living without appropriating means not allowing material considerations to prevent us going beyond our limits. It means taking risks in God's name, for God's name, but it does not only refer to material objects. Living without appropriating touches every part of our life, from placing all that we have in God's hands to all that we do and all that we are. Nothing is ours – our will, our good works, our anger over injustices done to us – we may keep none of it for our own benefit but must give it back to God who first lent it to us. Living a life of Franciscan poverty means surrendering ourselves to the will of God. We need not be afraid of enjoying God's gifts but we must always bear them lightly and be ready to share them or give them away.

The supper that Jesus shared with his friends the night before he died is, of course, at the heart of the Christian faith. Within it, we find the promise of life, given freely and abundantly. A life that is so rich that all the world cannot contain it, a life that is so small and humble it can be hidden in a piece of bread and some wine.

EXERCISE

Do today one thing that gives you pleasure, that costs nothing. It might be taking a walk in the countryside, in a park, or along a vibrant, busy street. It could be having a long relaxing bath, reading a book, playing with a child or a pet, or having a conversation with someone you love. Take time to enjoy your surroundings, your life, without needing to add to the material goods with which you are already burdened. Cherish the moment, not pausing to analyse your enjoyment but simply delighting in it. Treat the time as a precious gift, and sit lightly to the resources of the world as you do so.

GOOD FRIDAY

May I be happy
MATTHEW 27.27–37

Then the soldiers of the governor took Jesus into the governor's headquarters, and they gathered the whole cohort around him. They stripped him and put a scarlet robe on him, and after twisting some thorns into a crown, they put it on his head. They put a reed in his right hand and knelt before him and mocked him, saying, 'Hail, King of the Jews!' They spat on him, and took the reed and struck him on the head. After mocking him, they stripped him of the robe and put his own clothes on him. Then they led him away to crucify him.

As they went out, they came upon a man from Cyrene named Simon; they compelled this man to carry his cross. And when they came to a place called Golgotha (which means Place of a Skull), they offered him wine to drink, mixed with gall; but when he tasted it, he would not drink it. And when they had crucified him, they divided his clothes among themselves by casting lots; then they sat down there and kept watch over him. Over his head they put the charge against him, which read, 'This is Jesus, the King of the Jews.'

Crucifixion is a horrible, horrifying, agonizing death. Often prolonged and drawn out, the person hanging on a cross, perhaps with nails through their wrists and ankles, perhaps tied to the cross with ropes, would be forced to pull themselves upwards with their arms in order to breathe, a truly painful experience.

They might die from heart failure or asphyxiation if they were lucky – the less fortunate died slowly from dehydration, sepsis from the preceding scourging, or from attacks by the animals that prowled around the place of execution. It would be difficult to imagine a more humiliating and painful death, and its true nature is often hidden by the natural tendency to gloss over the appalling details. But it was this manner of death that Jesus willingly underwent in order to redeem us. It was this path that he chose to take in order that we need not walk down a similar path alone. It was for our sakes, every one of us, that he underwent such great suffering.

When faced with this scale of sacrificial suffering we can choose how we approach it. We can ignore it, turning our heads away from it, hiding away from the pain, pretending that it was not as great as it was. We can agonize over our own unworthiness, the impossibility of ever living up to such a sacrifice, the hopelessness of being worthy of such self-denying action. Or we can look with open eyes and full understanding on the cross, accepting the love that flows out from it towards us. We can be aware that we will never deserve such love, but aware too that we never need to, as by Christ's very action we no longer need to seek redemption through our own efforts, having been accorded it freely through the grace of God. We can resolve to live in the light of such love, able to meet the events of our life with equanimity, secure in the knowledge of Christ's saving action, content to greet each moment as it occurs, without fear or anxiety but confident in our ability to cope with it and live through it.

EXERCISE

Find a place to be still and quiet. Make yourself comfortable, either sitting or lying, with your eyes open or closed, as you prefer. Still your mind and body, using the three-minute breathing exercise. Then simply picture yourself resting in

God's arms. You can imagine yourself as a small child or as the fully grown person you are now. Imagine the sensations of being held by God; the warmth and comfort of his arms, the security of his grasp. Imagine his great love for you surrounding and enveloping you in its forgiving warmth and understanding. Pray for yourself, that you may remain aware of God's great love for you, and his peace that is always available to you. Try to set aside your concerns about yourself and what you do, who you are, and instead simply enjoy being in God's presence. You could pray on an in breath: 'May I find peace' or 'May I be happy' or simply 'God is with me'. Try not to let your mind dwell on your actions or words, simply on the fact of being a child of God, God's creation. When you are ready, focus again on the sensation of the breath entering and leaving your body.

HOLY SATURDAY

Wait in silence
PSALM 62.1-7

For God alone my soul waits in silence;
from him comes my salvation.
He alone is my rock and my salvation,
my fortress; I shall never be shaken.
How long will you assail a person,
will you batter your victim, all of you,
as you would a leaning wall, a tottering fence?
Their only plan is to bring down a person of prominence.
They take pleasure in falsehood;
they bless with their mouths,
but inwardly they curse.

For God alone my soul waits in silence,
for my hope is from him.
He alone is my rock and my salvation,
my fortress; I shall not be shaken.
On God rests my deliverance and my honour;
my mighty rock, my refuge is in God.

This psalm was written by King David at a time when not only his power, but his life itself, was threatened. Surrounded by enemies on all sides who were jealous of his position as king and envious of the popularity and success he enjoyed, David felt completely under siege from the forces of evil. Yet, interestingly, this is one of the few psalms that does not actually contain a prayer in it. Nowhere in this magnificent, confident, serene piece is a single exhortation uttered to God. In other psalms God is begged, pleaded with, to release the sufferer from their pains; God is beseeched to show mercy for past sins; he is praised for his glory. Yet in this one, written at a time of extreme crisis, there is nothing like that. Instead, there is a glorious confidence that God will protect David from all harm. Not containing a prayer, it is yet a psalm full of prayer for his life itself is dedicated to God. Not for him the shaky uncertainty of depending on systems or structures created by human beings, not for him the vagaries of trusting in other people for support or comfort. Instead, David relies on God alone as his rock and his salvation, confident that in God he will never be shaken.

Instead of being agitated about his future, and struggling to find a way out of an unpleasant and deeply frightening situation, David instead is content to 'wait in silence' for his God to deliver him, as he knows he will. Instead of anxiously turning events over in his mind, playing and replaying different possible outcomes, he is still, his heart fixed on God, silent, his soul waiting for the end to suffering that he knows will come. So too can we, when faced with a difficult, threatening or even frightening situation, learn to wait in silence for the deliverance that comes from God. Instead of allowing ourselves to become churned up inside, looking everywhere for a possible alternative situation, we can simply wait, trusting in God and his never-ending love and pity for us in our anxious and confused state.

EXERCISE

For almost 2,000 years, Christians have tried to practise the habit of unceasing prayer, using the name of Jesus as a foundation for their soul's longing. Eastern Christianity in particular employs the constant invocation of Jesus' name as a way of praying continually. The most well-known of these short prayers, and the one that has found its way most readily into Western Christianity, is that which is commonly called the 'Jesus Prayer': 'Lord Jesus Christ, Son of God, have mercy on me, a sinner'. This prayer centres on the figure of Christ, through whom we have been promised that all our prayers will be answered. It acknowledges the Trinity, as Jesus is acclaimed as Son of God by the Holy Spirit that dwells within us; and it calls for divine mercy for each one of us in our mortal, sinful state, confident that this call will be answered through the grace of God.

Find a place to be still and quiet. Make yourself comfortable, either sitting or lying, with your eyes open or closed, as you prefer. Still your mind and body, using the three-minute breathing exercise. Then with careful attention and concentration, repeat the Jesus Prayer in silence. You can use your breath to separate the phrases, breathing in with 'Lord Jesus Christ, Son of God' and breathing out for 'have mercy on me, a sinner'. Don't worry if your attention drifts away from what you are saying – simply notice that it has and draw your attention gently back to the prayer. When you are ready, focus again on the sensation of the breath entering and leaving your body.

EASTER SUNDAY

The effect of righteousness
ISAIAH 32.16–20

Then justice will dwell in the wilderness,
and righteousness abide in the fruitful field.
The effect of righteousness will be peace,
and the result of righteousness, quietness and trust for ever.
My people will abide in a peaceful habitation,
in secure dwellings, and in quiet resting places.
The forest will disappear completely,
and the city will be utterly laid low.
Happy will you be who sow beside every stream,
who let the ox and the donkey range freely.

Once again the prophet is looking forward to the time of the Messiah. And once again there is a great emphasis laid upon the concept of peace. Interestingly, it is not just human beings who will profit from the arrival of God's kingdom upon earth; the whole of creation will be transformed. The effect of sin will no more be seen on this planet, but instead everything will be renewed and restored to its original self. The wilderness will not be a place of fear and isolation, the place where outcasts dwell, those who live on the fringes of society, alienated from human company by their own actions or those of others. Instead, justice will transform its ferocity and it will no longer be a place to be feared. Those areas of land that are cultivated for crops will be 'fruitful' – no longer will people have to worry about the possibility of a poor harvest, for plentiful food will be available for everyone. Righteousness will abide in these fields, the righteousness that stems from doing what God requires, seeking to live the way God wants us to, fulfilling our potential as human beings in the unique and positive way that only we can achieve, with the grace of God, through prayer and right living. The result of this righteousness, we are promised, will be peace, the peace that comes from knowing we are doing God's will, the peace that comes from a complete trust in God and his loving purposes for us.

As Christians, we know that Christ's death and resurrection has brought God's kingdom here among us, right now. It is also yet to come, and we look forward to that time when all creation is reconciled through Christ. We live in the tension of the now and the not yet – our concern is to find the peace of God by focusing on the 'now', which will in its turn bring closer the 'not yet' of perfect redemption. Surrounded by frenetic activity and empty noise, we search for peace among the busyness of our lives, unaware that simply pausing for a few moments to savour the blessings of creation will bring us within reach of that peace which we long for so much.

EXERCISE

Supply yourself with a small piece of chocolate, and find a time when you can be sure of being undisturbed for a few minutes. Settle yourself so that you can be comfortable and still for several minutes, relaxed but alert, ready to focus, and prepared to turn your mind to the activity of the moment. Pick up the chocolate and examine it closely. Notice the way the light reflects off its surface, notice the difference in colour between the various areas of the chocolate. Notice the place where it was broken or where it came from the mould. Roll it gently between your fingers, being sensitive to the different sensations you are feeling. Notice how the chocolate reacts to the gentle pressure of your fingers, how it softens as it is warmed by your fingers. Hold it close to your nose, taking in some slow, deep breaths, allowing its fragrance to reach to the back of your throat. Notice the reaction of your mouth and the rest of your body to the smell of food. Carefully and thoughtfully place the chocolate on your tongue, holding it in your mouth for a few moments, rolling it on your tongue, feeling with your tongue what you felt previously with your fingers. Bite into it, sensing its texture against your teeth, noticing its taste in various parts of your mouth. When you have finished chewing, swallow carefully, being aware of the many different muscles in your mouth and throat that make up the swallowing action. When you have swallowed the chocolate, notice how the after-taste lingers on your tongue and in your mouth. Breathe slowly and deeply, remembering how tiny and insignificant a piece of chocolate is within the context of the universe. Then think of all the ingredients that went into its creation, and all of God's love that went into creating those ingredients. Remind yourself that God loves you, that all his love for all creation was poured out in creating you, redeeming you for his own.

The Mindful Pilgrimage

INTRODUCTION

For many people, a pilgrimage – a spiritual journey to a sacred place – is the ultimate exercise in mindfulness. Journeying on foot, aware of the gradual changes in the surrounding landscape, spending hours alone or in the company of a few people, carrying all that is required on one's back, pilgrimage has the effect of reducing one's entire life to the moment itself, as it is fully inhabited by the need purely to continue on the journey, to reach the destination. From the earliest times, people have made pilgrimages – evidence of aboriginal sacred journeys exists from prehistoric times and the pagan shrine of Apollo at Delphi was visited by the Ancient Greeks. For the

Jewish people, life as a sacred journey was a recurring theme, and the impetus for pilgrimage was carried over into Christian civilization. Eager to see and touch places where Christ was physically present, there is evidence from the fourth century of pilgrimages to Jerusalem. St Helena journeyed to Jerusalem in 326 and gathered lots of relics that she brought back with her, and from 385 we have the first pilgrim's guide book, *Peregrinatio egeriae*. By the beginning of the Middle Ages, pilgrimage was a fundamental part of European Christian life. Reasons for pilgrimage were many, and although not all pilgrims undertook the difficult and dangerous journey that was a pilgrimage for all of these reasons, behind every such excursion lay at least one reason. Many sought healing; some wanted forgiveness for past sins; others had the desire to see the places they had only read about; and still others yearned for the simple joy of journeying, in the hope that on the road their relationship with God might be deepened and strengthened.

Pilgrimage remains popular today, although more often as an end in itself – the journeying to a sacred place is enough. But experiences and encounters along the road and the arrival become the significant events, the channel through which deeper spiritual understanding can be arrived at. However, it must be remembered that the concept that was inherited by the medieval Church was that of physical pilgrimage as a metaphor for the place of human beings on earth. It is no longer necessary to find God in a particular place – thanks to the life, death and resurrection of Christ; God is now incarnate and can be found everywhere. Pilgrimage for Christians can thus become a metaphor for the journey of Christian living that has as its already anticipated goal the heavenly Jerusalem. This concept both relegates and elevates the role of pilgrimage within Christian spiritual practice. Pilgrimage itself has no intrinsic value – God cannot be found on a journey any more easily than he can be found in stillness. However, it can be used to understand more clearly our own situations and to re-inhabit them more deeply: physical pilgrimage can act as a symbol of the human journey which takes place through territory that is inhabited but not owned by human beings, and can be further employed to rededicate all places to their original purpose of glorifying their creator.

Pilgrimage is a physical response to an often unspoken need to journey towards a sacred centre, to explore a closer relationship with the creator and the created, finding within the exploration a place for the self.

EXERCISE

Consider going on a pilgrimage – if you have never undertaken such a journey before, you might want to begin with a simple day trip to a local church. Decide upon your destination, making sure first of all that the place will be open, and work out a suitable starting point – this does not have to be your own home but can be somewhere you travel to first before beginning your pilgrimage. You also need to decide how you will return home once your destination has been reached. Aim to walk between 10 and 12 miles at about 2½ miles an hour if you are an inexperienced walker, although if you are used to travelling by foot you may wish to make the journey longer. Take with you plenty of food and water, suitable clothing to protect you from the elements, whether wind, rain or sun, a map if you need one, a simple first aid kit and a good pair of shoes. Decide whether you wish to journey with a companion or travel alone, set a date and then simply take the first step!

If a day-long walk is too much to undertake at the present time, there are other ways of making a journey in the spirit of the pilgrimage.

Travelling lightly
LUKE 10.1–4

> *After this the Lord appointed seventy others and sent them on ahead of him in pairs to every town and place where he himself intended to go. He said to them, 'The harvest is plentiful, but the labourers are few; therefore ask the Lord of the harvest to send out labourers into his harvest. Go on your way. See, I am sending you out like lambs into the midst of wolves. Carry no purse, no bag, no sandals; and greet no one on the road.*

One of the greatest challenges when planning a pilgrimage is not deciding on your route, nor how long you will journey for, nor even where you will stay – the most fraught decisions occur when thinking about what to pack. On the road, the seasoned pilgrim can always be spotted not only because of the weather-beaten nature of their kit, but also because of its size – the more experienced the traveller, the smaller the size of their backpack! A new pilgrim might avidly read the pages of advice on such ventures that are available on the website, poring over discussion forums debating which waterproof is best, or how many spare pairs of socks to take. Anyone who has made a pilgrimage before will know that the best luggage is the lightest. Heavy packs, weighed down with things that might come in useful, may give a spurious sense of confidence to the inexperienced walker, making them feel secure in the knowledge that they are prepared for any eventuality. However, the very weight of the pack heralds its own downfall – the pilgrim will travel more slowly, become tired more quickly, may get more and larger blisters, and so become liable to the very eventualities that they have prepared against. Better by far to travel as the earliest pilgrims did, with as little as possible, save only the bare necessities. Sound advice this, with one exception – many people, once they have put in the essentials, will then include a few items that could be termed luxuries, but in fact will simply make the journey more pleasurable for the pilgrim. These items are as individual as the people who carry them – special teabags perhaps, a favourite book, a bottle of sauce guaranteed to transform the blandest of meals. Not in themselves necessary, they bring an additional, personal dimension to the journey.

On our own journey through life, there is a grave danger of becoming so weighed down with both physical and mental baggage that our progress is made unnecessarily slow and difficult. One of the spiritual exercises we can undertake periodically is to conduct a review of those attitudes and assumptions that we take for granted that we do not, however, need to carry with us.

EXERCISE

You might wish to gather a handful of stones before beginning this exercise. They can be a useful aid to visualization and help you appreciate the nature of your burdens.

Look at the things you want to take with you on your journey into the rest of your life. See them as reflections of the spiritual things you are taking. Some of these spiritual objects are like bricks – totally unnecessary, serving only to make the pack burdensome. Are you taking with you a materialist anxiety, a concern that what you have might not be enough, or might reflect badly on you? Are you taking with you unnecessary regrets, from childhood or from last week? Are you carrying feelings that block an attitude of thanksgiving and hopefulness?

Determine to take with you only the important things – your beliefs, your love for those with whom you share your life, a generous spirit and an open heart.

Imagine yourself setting out on a journey, by foot. If it helps, picture in your mind a favourite walk, or a place you have visited. You are taking nothing with you, no handbag or wallet, certainly no backpack or suitcase. There is simply you and the route ahead. Imagine yourself shutting your front door behind you and striding out on the first stage of your journey. How does this feel? Are you anxious about the fact that you have nothing with you in case of emergencies, or do you feel inexplicably light and carefree? Are you worried about how you will manage, or are you confident that you will be able to cope with any event that arises on your trip? If you are feeling worried by the thought of a journey undertaken with so little preparation, make a conscious effort to turn around your thinking into one of joyful anticipation of the route ahead. Remind yourself of Jesus' instructions to his disciples and the wonderful way that his promises came true – shelter found, provision made, people healed. Even times of difficulty and trouble were to be met with the carefree confidence that comes with a reliance on God.

Now think about the rest of your life, and consider the luggage that you carry with you on this journey. Using your handful of stones, first make a small pile of those essential items that cannot be 'put down' – a dependent relative, perhaps, an illness or disability, a vital relationship. Make the number of stones as small as possible.

Look at this pile of stones and thank God for all that it contains. Ask God to use these burdens that you carry to fulfil his purposes for you. Ask him for his help in carrying them and for faith to journey on when the weight of them seems too much to bear. Pray for his love to flow through you in such a way that all that these stones represent may be used to the glory of his kingdom.

Use more stones to create another, larger pile, to

represent those burdens that you carry with you that you do not need to take. These might include feelings of guilt over a failed relationship, regret over unsatisfactory life choices, a dependence on material objects for feelings of acceptance, or an addiction to a particular food or drink, however harmless.

Looking at these stones, consider the unnecessary weight that they represent. Ask for God's help in leaving these burdens behind. Resolve to put damaging thoughts and feelings to one side, leaving them behind with the stones as you continue on your way, focusing your mind on the way ahead.

Living in the moment
PSALM 118.19–24, 28–29

Open to me the gates of righteousness,
that I may enter through them
and give thanks to the Lord.

This is the gate of the Lord;
the righteous shall enter through it.
I thank you that you have answered me
and have become my salvation.
The stone that the builders rejected
has become the chief cornerstone.
This is the Lord's doing;
it is marvellous in our eyes.
This is the day that the Lord has made;
let us rejoice and be glad in it …
You are my God, and I will give thanks to you;
you are my God, I will extol you.
O give thanks to the Lord, for he is good,
for his steadfast love endures for ever.

I knew the man was a novice pilgrim because of the size of his backpack. A tall man, this pack still towered above him, clanking with extra objects that had been lashed to the outside, bulging with stuff, sparkling in its newness. By rights he should have had that look of dazed fatigue that is common to many walkers on their first sustained journey, but instead his eyes were shining and his face was lit up with excitement. He greeted me in rapid French, which slowed down only just enough for me to understand it, so eager was he to share his thoughts and emotions on this experience. A lifelong city dweller, the profound peace and lush greenery of the Burgundy countryside had hit him like a lightning bolt – he couldn't believe the variety of plants and trees that surrounded him on his walk, and he marvelled at the tiny details of the landscape that unfolded slowly and gradually over the course of the day. He was a joy to walk with, and a reminder that not one moment of our lives should be taken for granted, or spent on pointless regret or needless anticipation, but instead cherished to the full, every drop of life wrung from it. Unless we take great care, we can spend our 'now' looking forwards or backwards, but never fully engaged in the moment, measuring out our life journey in days ahead or past, not giving ourselves the gift of immersion in the present. Today is all that we truly have, and this day is sacred to God – 'this is the day that the Lord has made – let us rejoice and be glad in it'. Now is the time to relish every moment, savour every encounter and experience. Part of the focus of our journey will inevitably involve reflection, and integration of past experiences.

> *Only when you have gone deeply into the experience of the moment, of the precise instant in which we are alive, day by day, hour by hour, second by second, will we be able to experience the infinite. True freedom lies in learning to pay attention to the infinite detail that makes up each moment of our lives, allowing us to experience them in a new way. Our*

mindfulness enables us to live each day, each hour, as a new beginning, and to continue to face the future with an open heart and mind.

Sally Welch, *Making a Pilgrimage*, Lion Hudson, 2009

EXERCISE

Although hopefully part of your preparation for pilgrimage will have involved spending some time in training, preparing for a very demanding piece of physical work, it is possible that the first few days of your journey will be quite taxing. For much of our daily lives, it is possible to remain unaware of our physical bodies, noticing them only when they complain in the form of pain or discomfort at the burdens that are placed on them. Unused to sustained physical exercise, the discipline of sustained walking – hours each day, days at a time, through periods of fatigue, pulled muscles and blisters – will give us a renewed awareness of our bodies and our relationship with them. Once the initial shock has disappeared, however, and we have become acclimatized to physical exertion, we can feel a new enjoyment in our bodily wellbeing, uncomplicated and direct, liberating and exciting. There will be moments when we are completely at ease with our body, rejoicing in its strength, grateful for the gift of its creation.

When walking and resting, take time out to be aware of your body, to celebrate it, and be grateful even for the parts you don't particularly like! Feeling good in your skin is a gift from the road – enjoy it.

Take some time to make your journey particularly mindful. Walk slowly and purposefully to your chosen place, aware of every movement that your body makes, celebrating its ability to make such actions. Try and focus your attention on different parts of your body as you walk, concentrating first on your feet and the sensation of walking on the ground, the type of surface, and the feeling of this underfoot. Move your attention slowly upwards, feeling your calf and thigh muscles stretch and contract as you take each stop, the action of your chest as it draws breath, your arms by your side or gently swinging in time with each pace. If any part of your body registers discomfort or pain, notice this, and stay with it briefly, inhabiting that part of the body without concerning yourself overmuch; simply registering the feeling. On your arrival at your destination, spend some time in silence, in a posture that is comfortable and relaxed, feeling the sensation of fabric, wood, stone, against parts of your body, allowing your mind the space simply to be, a child of God, loved by God, in all your bodily form, with all its personal characteristics and idiosyncrasies. You might want to use your breathing prayer (see page 6), or even a whole body scan (page 8), during your time in silence.

When you have spent as long as you need or are able, return home slowly and mindfully once more, focusing on the feelings of movement and acknowledging your place in the environment that you travel through.

Encountering obstacles
JOSHUA 1.1–2, 5B–7, 9

After the death of Moses the servant to the Lord, the Lord spoke to Joshua son of Nun, Moses' assistant, saying, 'My servant Moses is dead. Now proceed to cross the Jordan, you and all this people, into the land that I am giving to them, to the Israelites …

'As I was with Moses so I will be with you; I will not fail you or forsake you. Be strong and courageous; for you shall put this people in possession of the land that I swore to their

ancestors to give them. Only be strong and very courageous, being careful to act in accordance with all the law that my servant Moses commanded you; do not turn from it to the right hand or to the left, so that you may be successful wherever you go …

'I hereby command you: Be strong and courageous; do not be frightened or dismayed, for the Lord your God is with you wherever you go.'

My most frightening experience when on pilgrimage occurred when I was walking on my own through the middle of France. I had been walking along a forest track for over an hour, and had gone about 2½ miles. On looking at my map, I discovered that I still had a further 2½ miles to travel before I would emerge from the densely wooded area. On looking around I noticed that it was incredibly quiet – there were no bird sounds, not even the rustling of leaves in the breeze to disturb the silence. I was overcome with an enormous fear – of what I could not be specific, but all sorts of human, animal and even supernatural dangers rushed through my mind. I texted my husband: 'All alone in middle of forest with still one hour to travel to safety.' From his office in Oxford came the reply: 'Think Little Red Riding Hood!' By rights, this allusion to the fairy tale adventure of the girl who travels through the woods on the way to her grandmother's house, only to be devoured by a wolf, should have appalled me by its heartlessness. Instead, I found it tremendously reassuring, reducing as it did my nameless fears to what they really were – groundless worries based on a fevered imagination. Cheered, I continued on my way, reaching the end of the forest in complete safety.

Too often our reactions to events and situations in our life are coloured by our experiences of the past. When faced with a new situation, we trawl through our memories and our imaginations to find previous experiences, and from them extrapolate possible future scenarios. Although the benefit of experience and the wisdom accumulated through lifetimes should not be ignored, none the less it is not always helpful to mistake our thoughts and feelings for reality. Experiences can be valuable but only if they are recognized as tools for dealing with the present, rather than real-life predictors of what will occur. Better still to focus not on anxieties but actualities, to explore events that are actually occurring rather than ones that we fear will unfold.

EXERCISE

Find a quiet and secluded spot, where you can be confident that you will remain undisturbed for as long as you need to be. Make sure you feel supported and balanced in your body, relaxed but alert. Close your eyes if this helps. Take some time to 'take notice' of what is happening in your mind right now. You don't need to comment on it or judge or decide on any action, simply be aware of the thoughts and worries that are churning about. Do not allow yourself to become engaged with them; just observe them.

Instead of letting all your fears scramble themselves around in your head, you might find it helpful instead to take a piece of paper and write them down in a list.

Look at the list, and examine how you feel about seeing them in black and white – sometimes the simple act of writing them down reduces their power.

Choose one fear that still has power over you; one that you find difficulty in simply observing but instead sends your mind chasing after possible scenarios, and write this down on a new piece of paper. Beneath this fear, write how you would behave if you did not have this fear, and how it would affect your life.

Scrunch the paper up in your hands, while you determine to act as if you were free of this fear, and behave as if you were well able to deal with the events that make you afraid.

Now move your attention back to your breath, feeling

---

it enter and leave your body, filling your body with life. Focus on the breath as it moves in and out. If your mind wanders, do not become anxious or concerned, simply take notice and return to the breath, in and out.

You may find it helpful to repeat God's words to Joshua: 'Be strong and courageous; do not be frightened or dismayed, for the Lord your God is with you wherever you go.'

Sharing with strangers
ACTS 8.26–31A, 35–39

Then an angel of the Lord said to Philip, 'Get up and go towards the south to the road that goes down from Jerusalem to Gaza.' (This is a wilderness road.) So he got up and went. Now there was an Ethiopian eunuch, a court official of the Candace, queen of the Ethiopians, in charge of her entire treasury. He had come to Jerusalem to worship and was returning home, seated in his chariot, he was reading the prophet Isaiah. Then the Spirit said to Philip, 'Go over to this chariot and join it.' So Philip ran up to it and heard him reading the prophet Isaiah. He asked, 'Do you understand what you are reading?' He replied, 'How can I, unless someone guides me?' ...

Then Philip began to speak, and starting with this scripture, he proclaimed to him the good news about Jesus. As they were going along the road, they came to some water; and the eunuch said, 'Look, here is water! What is to prevent me from being baptized?' He commanded the chariot to stop, and both of them, Philip and the eunuch, went down into the water, and Philip baptized him. When they came up out of the water, the Spirit of the Lord snatched Philip away; the eunuch saw him no more, and went on his way rejoicing.

131

One of the joys of travelling on pilgrimage is the encounters with those you meet along the way – fellow travellers, hospitality providers, other road users, and the inhabitants of the settlements you walk through. On the less popular routes, particularly, there is a genuine feeling of support and encouragement from the local community for the task you are undertaking. The special nature of the journey is recognized and given value – I have been asked to take prayers with me, and people have stopped me and told me they would pray for me. Even a cheerful wave from a passing motorist does much to lift the spirits during a tiring part of the journey; a reminder that this journey, although it might be taken alone, is not a lonely one.

Many thousands of people, before and since, will walk the same route, for different reasons, in different ways, but with the same trust in the gift of the journey. Chance encounters and generous offers of hospitality, however small, enrich the moment and develop a new trust in the essential goodness of human beings. Fellow travellers also bring a new and entrancing dimension to aspects of the journey – eccentric, brave, fearless, strange figures walking through the landscape, each bearing their own burden but many times prepared to bear the burdens of others as well. But we must be prepared to engage with these encounters, open to what they will bring, prepared to accept new ways of thinking and looking, while sharing our own thoughts and feelings. Just as Philip can get nowhere with the Ethiopian until he takes that first brave step of getting inside the Ethiopian's chariot and actually travelling alongside him, reading what he reads and sharing the experience, so too our relationships with others will always be shallow and clouded while they are viewed through the distorting lens of our own personal viewpoint. We must put aside our own judgements, our prejudices, and genuinely listen to the tales of the ones with whom we are travelling, or who we encounter on the road. We need to stop bringing our own preconceptions to our meetings and encounters, cease to label them according to our own personal world view, and accept our connectedness with the whole of humankind through Jesus Christ. In a similar way, we need to learn how not to depend upon others for our own sense of value and identity. Our identity comes from within and we do not need to define ourselves either positively or negatively through others. Only when we are free from this need will we be truly free to serve God and our neighbour in the most appropriate way.

EXERCISE

Take two glasses of drinking water. Into one put a spoonful of mud or soil and mix it up. Notice how the water becomes cloudy and dirty, how it is difficult to see through the glass, which itself becomes soiled with the mud. So too are our thoughts and perceptions when we allow past experiences and episodes to cloud our judgements, preventing us from seeing new encounters clearly and objectively. Far better to offer a drink of cool, clear water to a friend or stranger, free from prejudice and with the clarity of wisdom and truth better able by far to listen and engage, exploring relationships and deepening love.

Rest and restoration
PSALM 16.1–11

Protect me, O God, for in you I take refuge.
I say to the Lord, 'You are my Lord;
I have no good apart from you.'
As for the holy ones in the land, they are the noble,
in whom is all my delight.
Those who choose another god multiply their sorrows;
their drink-offerings of blood I will not pour out
or take their names upon my lips.

The Lord is my chosen portion and my cup;
you hold my lot.
The boundary lines have fallen for me in pleasant places;
I have a goodly heritage.

I bless the Lord who gives me counsel;
in the night also my heart instructs me.
I keep the Lord always before me;
because he is at my right hand, I shall not be moved.
Therefore my heart is glad, and my soul rejoices;
my body also rests secure.
For you do not give me up to Sheol,
or let your faithful one see the Pit.

You show me the path of life.
In your presence there is fullness of joy;
in your right hand are pleasures for evermore.

It is easy to spot them – those determined pilgrims whose main aim seems to be to accomplish the journey as quickly as possible. Those people whose goal is the destination, and who will not be diverted from that goal. They walk quickly, often with their heads down, as if not only their backpacks, but their thoughts and feelings as well, weighed them down. They do not deviate from the path no matter how enticing the roadside inn or enchanting the small churches and shrines that are scattered along the edges of pilgrim paths like pearls on a string, showing the way to the main jewel of the principal site. They can be seen at night, in the hostels, poring over the map for the following day, learning the route so that they do not have to delay their journey by stopping to open up the guide book. Often their feet are bloody and bandaged, as large blisters appear and are broken under the pressure of high-speed walking. But not even this deters them or prevents them from adhering to their rigid timetable – so many miles an hour, so many miles per day, until the destination is reached. What anxiety is there in their hearts, that they cannot release themselves, even for a moment, from their task! What fears drive them, leaving them unable to deviate from the prescribed route! How different is the joyous faith of the psalmist, who, although he acknowledges his terrors, his fears of Sheol and the Pit, has decided to place all his trust firmly in God, and so experiences the complete joy and freedom that is the result of his decision. The psalmist is free to wander slowly in the 'pleasant places', enjoying the 'goodly heritage' that has been given to him by a creator God who rejoices in every tiny detail of his creation. The psalmist is glad, his soul 'rejoices', and he finds a secure rest through his faith in an everloving God, who has provided for him in the past, and will certainly not abandon him in the future.

Many times on pilgrimage and in our lives also, we have a strong urge to focus solely on our goals, pressing ahead regardless of the physical and emotional landscape that surrounds us. Driven perhaps by fear of failure, or fear of an unimaginable chaos that might descend if we deviate from the path we have chosen, we live our lives looking always to a future, often fearful of that future, rarely confident in our hoped-for outcome. Where is the kindness that we try so hard to show to others? We need to apply this to ourselves, our minds and our bodies. We need to use the empathy and compassion that we pour out upon those with whom we share our lives when we deal with our own lives, allowing ourselves moments of weakness, of anxiety, of stress, without becoming controlled by those feelings, pausing to rest and reflect when we need to, driven not by our inner timetable or the timetables of others, but by our soul's agenda, that of loving God, our neighbour and ourselves.

EXERCISE

Find a quiet space, outside if at all possible, one that is warm and dry, so that you can be completely relaxed and comfortable. Find a space that is wide and open, ideally with a view of the countryside, but at the least surrounded by trees and greenery. If you cannot be outside, choose somewhere with large windows looking out on to a pleasant landscape. Lie down on the grass, and focus on the sensations you feel in each part of your body where it touches the ground – perhaps a hardness against your back and head, or a tickling where the grass rubs against your skin. Be aware of your breathing, and beginning with your toes, try to discern any sensation or feeling in them. Don't worry if you feel nothing, sometimes this comes with continued practice of the body scan. If you experience discomfort in your toes, notice this. Try not to become involved in analysing the sensation or worrying about it; simply notice it without judging, allowing it to be what it is.

Deepen your breathing, becoming aware of your breath flowing throughout your entire body, filling every blood cell with oxygen, sustaining life.

Gradually move your attention from your toes to your feet, then to the lower and upper parts of your legs. Steadily and slowly, focus on each part of your body in turn, resting your attention on it for ten or twenty seconds, without deliberately counting the time, simply pausing long enough to register the sensations that you feel. If you experience tension or pain, breathe into them, exploring the feeling, allowing your mind to register the feeling without judging it, simply noticing it, before moving on.

Don't worry if your mind wanders – it probably will. When it does, simply bring it back to the task in hand, the task of the present, and continue your journey round your body.

After you have scanned your whole body, continue breathing in silence. You may wish to breathe in part of Psalm 16: '... my heart is glad, and my soul rejoices; my body also rests secure.'